ONE WOK, ONE POT

KWOKLYN WAN

ONE WOK, ONE POT

Fuss-free and delicious dishes using only one pot

Photography by Sam Folan
Illustrations by Adam Hayes

Hardie Grant

QUADRILLE

Managing Director Sarah Lavelle
Commissioning Editor Stacey Cleworth
Designer Alicia House
Photographer Sam Folan
Food Stylist Katie Marshall
Props Stylist Agathe Gits
Cover Typography Adam Hayes
Head of Production Stephen Lang
Senior Production Controller Sabeena Atchia

Published in 2023 by Quadrille
an imprint of Hardie Grant Publishing

Quadrille
52–54 Southwark Street
London SE1 1UN
quadrille.com

Cataloguing in Publication Data: a catalogue record
for this book is available from the British Library.

Text © Kwoklyn Wan 2023
Photography © Quadrille 2023
Design © Quadrille 2023
Cover Typography © Adam Hayes 2023

ISBN 9781787139084

Printed in China

22.

82.

121.

149.

INTRODUCTION

Most cultures across the globe have their own version of a one-pot meal, contributing to a worldwide collection of dishes to tease and tantalize that all share one simple defining factor – they are all prepared in one pot, be that a pan, slow cooker, rice cooker or wok!

Some hardcore devotees would insist that to be a true 'one-pot meal', all the elements of the meal must be cooked solely in one pot and that serving a side dish is cheating. Personally, I think it's open to interpretation. In my humble opinion, if one-pot cooking is all about ease and comfort, nothing whispers home-cooked satisfaction more than a lovingly prepared one-pot meal paired with a bowl of steamed rice or even a soft bread roll for dunking. Let's be honest, you wouldn't think twice about pairing your one-pot cup of tea with a cookie or two.

Influenced by my heritage and the many delicious East and Southeast Asian cuisines and flavours and regional specialities – from Japan and Korea to Thailand and Malaysia – I have designed the recipes in this book in the hopes of inspiring you to relax in your kitchen and get back to a simpler way of cooking, but as always, to never lose out on flavour and texture.

For those hectic households with after-school clubs competing with meal times, what easier way to satisfy the family than to have a ready-prepared pot bubbling away on the stove when the afternoon rush is over, so that everyone, including the household chef, can take a seat and enjoy the meal together; for the young professionals living life on the run, a slow-cooker meal prepared the night before and quickly flicked on in the morning before leaving for work will be a hearty smell to welcome them home at the end of a busy day; and for the humble student living in shared accommodation with only one pan to their name, pot rice and noodle bowls will keep them fed and probably quite popular amongst housemates.

One-pot cooking is all about keeping it simple: whether you're pressed for time or you just don't have the space and equipment for creating large meals, these recipes are the perfect space- and time-saving answer to pleasing your taste buds.

INGREDIENTS

Rice

There are so many different types to choose from. Jasmine rice is commonly used throughout China and is slightly fragrant, but you can use most long-grain varieties and some medium grains too. Long-grain varieties include basmati, jasmine, wild rice and American long-grain rice. While arborio, California calrose and Chinese black rice or 'Emperor's Rice' are all medium-grain.

In some of my dishes I use glutinous rice, which when cooked is very, very sticky. Though the name may suggest it contains gluten, it is in fact completely gluten-free. The name comes from the fact that when the grain is cooked it becomes like glue.

Rice noodles

Rice noodles are made from rice flour and water, but in some brands tapioca or cornflour (cornstarch) is used to improve elasticity and chewiness. You can buy rice noodles in varying thicknesses, from string-like noodles like vermicelli to thick, fat, flat noodles, which are normally referred to as ho fun.

Many supermarkets now sell the ready-to-wok noodles, but you can use the dried packet noodles too; simply rehydrate them in boiling water before using. Instructions are always on the packet so be sure to follow those.

Glass noodles

Glass noodles, also known as cellophane noodles, are a type of transparent noodle made from starch (such as mung bean starch, potato starch or tapioca starch). Used in stir-fries, soups and spring rolls, these noodles add texture and bite to a dish. Like rice noodles, you can buy these noodles dried and rehydrate them in boiling water when you need to use them.

Chinese sausage (lap cheong)

Lap cheong is a type of dried fatty sausage normally made from pork, though other varieties, including chicken and duck, are now available. Often eaten as part of dim sum and steamed or cooked inside rice parcels, the sausages are sweet, sometimes smoky and utterly delicious. The tradition of 'Dim Sum' began in ancient China where travellers along the old Silk Road broke up their journey by stopping at tea houses. As it was discovered that drinking tea aids digestion, small pieces of food were offered with the tea. In Cantonese this is referred to as 'Yum Cha' – which is the complete act of having a meal while drinking tea.

Garlic, ginger and spring onion – aka 'The Holy Trinity'

This threesome features heavily in Chinese cooking, and a dish would only truly be considered Cantonese with the inclusion of at least one, if not all three of the Holy Trinity of aromatics – garlic, ginger and spring onion.

Chilli paste

Doubanjiang: A Chinese chilli bean paste that is savoury and spicy, made from fermented broad beans, soya beans, flour, salt and chillies, which adds a complex flavour to the dishes it is cooked with. Throughout China there are different variations of the paste; the most well known is from Sichuan.

Gochujang: A Korean paste that is fundamental to many dishes. It is red in colour and made from chilli (red pepper) flakes, glutinous rice, fermented soya beans and salt. It has a rich flavour packed with umami.

Chilli powder

Chilli powders come in a range of heats so you and your dinner companions should consider which one to use. Some like it hot and some can barely handle the mere thought of spice, so where a recipe calls for chilli powder, use your favourite brand and heat level and, as you cook, always remember to taste and adjust the seasoning to your personal preference.

Light soy sauce

Light soy sauce is made from fermented soya beans and wheat; it has a strong aromatic umami and savoury flavour, making it ideal as a marinade, dressing, sauce and table condiment. Gluten-free soy sauce is also available from some brands.

Dark soy sauce

Fermented for a much longer time – to produce a rich, dark, sweeter sauce – dark soy sauce is packed with umami and is perfect for marinades and colouring your dishes. Look out for tamari for a gluten-free option.

Fish sauce

A liquid condiment made from salted fish which have been left to ferment for up to two years. Used as a seasoning in many East Asian countries, although more commonly in Thai and Filipino cooking, it's packed with umami. It can be used in cooking or after cooking as a dipping sauce.

Oyster sauce

Discovered by accident in 1888 when a boiling pot of oyster soup was forgotten on the stove and simmered away to a thick sauce, this is a flavour game changer with its irresistible umami saltiness. Vegetarians needn't miss out either, as mushroom stir-fry sauce is very similar in texture and, as it's made from dried shiitake mushrooms and seaweed, it still packs a great umami punch.

Hoisin sauce

A thick fragrant sauce made with fermented soya beans, most commonly used as a glaze for meats, a dipping condiment or as a stir-fry sauce.

White rice vinegar

Made from fermented rice, this type of vinegar is less acidic and sweeter than its malt-based counterparts. It is used in dressings, for seasoning dishes and in rice. Its closest alternative is cider vinegar.

Black rice vinegar

Made from black rice, this type of vinegar has a complex, slightly smoky flavour. It can be used as an ingredient or as a dipping condiment. It can also be used in sauces, stir-fries and soups.

Chinese rice wine

Shaoxing wine is a type of Chinese cooking wine, made from rice. It has a complex sweet flavour. A must-have ingredient and sadly a no-go for the gluten-free diner as there is a small quantity of wheat involved in the fermentation process.

Sesame oil

Add the tiniest amount of this oil to marinades or as a drizzle at the very end of cooking to transform your dish! Use sparingly as it's packed with flavour and can easily overpower if used too heavily. Where possible buy pure sesame oil and not the blended variety, and never cook with it; use only for marinating and seasoning.

Cooking oils

Oils with a higher smoke point lend themselves better to traditional Chinese cooking due to the high heat and fast cooking methods used. Suitable varieties that are readily available include vegetable oil, rapeseed oil, peanut (groundnut) oil and soya bean oil.

Cornflour (cornstarch)

Used to coat ingredients and create light crispy batters, massaged into meats to marinate and tenderize or mixed with a splash of water to create a sauce thickener, this finely textured starch is an all-rounder in Chinese cooking.

Chicken powder

Chicken bouillon powder is a pale yellow colour and used as a seasoning in many Chinese recipes. The flavour is salty and has a concentrated chicken stock taste, adding a rich umami flavour to a dish.

EQUIPMENT

Flameproof casserole

A type of cooking pot with a lid that can be used in the oven or on the hob (stove). The perfect pot to be used when cooking soups, stews, pot roasts and sauces. If you're a devoted home cook, you'll want to buy the best that you can as it will be used a lot. In terms of size, a 3–4-litre (13¼–17½-cup) casserole will suit most households.

Wok

Traditional woks were round-bottomed and would sit in a hollow above an open fire. Originating from China, similar pans to the wok are used widely in most East Asian countries. The design would concentrate the heat around the bottom of the wok making it very, very hot, which would cook the food quickly and in relatively very little oil. Modern versions are designed with a flat bottom so they are able to sit on your stove top, and most are now non-stick, which means you no longer need the intense heat to cook the food and can use less oil thanks to the non-stick surface. A 35cm (14in) wok would be suitable for the average household.

Clay pot

A piece of cookware that is created under high heat using clay. Clay pots are often glazed inside but unglazed on the outside. They come with a lid and sometimes with a wire frame, which helps to hold the shape of the pot when it expands during cooking. The design makes the pot porous – this allows the heat and moisture to circulate evenly when cooking, which helps food retain its nutrients. Meats cooked in a clay pot tend to be a lot juicier and more tender. A 3–4-litre (13¼–17½-cup) pot will work for the majority of recipes in this book.

In China and Hong Kong, the clay pot used for such cooking is generally known as *bōu jái*, which translates in Cantonese to 'little pot'. Clay pot dishes are often listed as 'Hot Pot' dishes on the menu of Chinese restaurants and, if spotted on a menu, I highly recommend the chicken, salt fish and Chinese mushrooms.

Rice cooker

An automated electrical cooker that has been designed to cook your rice. It has its own heat source and a bowl to cook the rice within. Wash your rice, add the correct measure of water, click on the cooker and let it do its thing! A 3–4-litre (13¼–17½-cup) capacity rice cooker will work for most home cooks.

Pressure cooker

Working on the simple principle of a sealed pot with a lot of steam inside, creating high pressure to help cook food faster. Meat is incredibly tender when cooked in a pressure cooker, removing the need to wait long hours for tougher cuts to achieve melt-in-the-mouth texture. Available in a variety of sizes, a 3–4-litre (13¼–17½-cup) pressure cooker should suit the average household.

Bamboo steamer

Bamboo steamers have been used in China for the last 5,000 years. They are still used widely, especially in the cooking and serving of dim sum. To use a steamer, simply place the food inside and then sit the steamer above a pan of boiling water – as the steam rises, the food is cooked in the moist heat.

Steamer baskets come in various sizes and can be chosen based on the quantity of food being steamed. The standard size is 25cm (10in) but consideration also needs to be given to the size of the pan that will sit under the basket; too large and the basket will fall in, too small and the steam will simply escape rather than being collected inside the basket to cook the food.

Baking tray/sheet

A baking tray or baking sheet is a multi-functional, usually rectangular pan used in the oven and can be useful for baking anything from chicken thighs to almond cookies. Usually utilized for drier baking.

Baking dish

Much like the baking tray/sheet but deeper and better suited for baking saucier dishes or roasting meats that will release a lot of juice.

Saucepans

Most kitchens will have an array of pans, from the spouted milk pan to the larger lidded saucepan. A deep saucepan or frying pan can be used as an alternative to a wok but the wider bottomed the better if you're going to substitute this piece of equipment.

What size to choose?

When choosing the size of any pan, wok or tray, always consider the amount of ingredients that you are going to be cooking in it, as well as the quantity of liquid that you'll be adding or that will be released from the fresh ingredients. You don't want the pan or dish to be so full that it's at risk of bubbling over or causing a burning spill over your hands when you lift it out of the oven at the end of cooking, so always make sure you give the ingredients room to breathe and move around.

STARTERS

SWEET CHILLI BACON BUNS

Salty yet sweet, sticky and crispy, creamy yet spicy; a whole world of flavour in a delicately buttery bun.

Prep 2 minutes
Cook 10 minutes
Serves 2

Equipment
Wok

1 tbsp salted butter
2 brioche buns
1 tbsp vegetable or sunflower oil
2 eggs
pinch of sea salt flakes
good pinch of chilli (red pepper) flakes
about 5 slices of streaky bacon
60ml (¼ cup) maple syrup
sweet chilli sauce, to serve

Add the butter to a hot wok and, once melted and foamy, cut the brioche buns in half and place cut-sides down into the butter. Fry for a couple of minutes until golden brown. Remove from the wok and place to one side, butter-side up.

Wipe the wok clean with kitchen paper, then add the oil and fry your eggs over a high heat, as you want them to have a crispy bottom. Once cooked to your liking, place one egg on top of the bottom toasted brioche bun and sprinkle with the sea salt flakes and chilli (red pepper) flakes.

Add the bacon to the hot wok, cook until golden brown and crispy, then pour in the maple syrup and continue to cook until the syrup is thickened and sticky. Arrange the syrupy bacon on top of the eggs and add a good blob of your sweet chilli sauce, then carefully place the top and bottom halves together to create brioche bun towers.

YELLOW BEAN PORK WRAPS

A lip-smackingly tasty Chinese twist on the Mexican burrito! Tender strips of pork dressed in a rich yellow bean sauce and wrapped in a cool, crisp iceberg leaf.

Prep 10 minutes
Cook 7 minutes
Serves 2

Equipment
Wok

1 iceberg lettuce
1 tbsp vegetable oil
1 garlic clove, minced
thumb-sized piece of ginger, peeled and cut into thin matchsticks
250g (9oz) pork tenderloin, cut into matchsticks
1 yellow (bell) pepper, deseeded and cut into matchsticks
3 spring onions (scallions), cut into 5cm (2in) lengths
2 tbsp yellow bean sauce, or hoisin sauce if preferred
1 tbsp light soy sauce
½ tbsp white rice vinegar
125ml (½ cup) chicken stock
1 tsp cornflour (cornstarch) mixed with 2 tsp water
handful of salted cashew nuts

Separate the lettuce leaves, trying to keep them intact; the best way of doing this is to hold the head of the lettuce by the stalk under a gently running cold tap, and as the leaves fill with water they peel (intact) away from the head.

Place a wok over a medium-high heat, add the oil along with the garlic and ginger, then after 20 seconds add the pork, give it all a quick stir and fry for 2 minutes. Add the yellow pepper and spring onions (scallions) and continue to fry for a further minute. Then add the yellow bean sauce, soy sauce, rice vinegar and stock. Once boiling, give your cornflour (cornstarch) mixture a mix and slowly stir into the sauce, a little at a time, until you have your desired consistency. Once thickened, turn off the heat, sprinkle over the cashew nuts, mix and serve with the iceberg leaves.

To eat, take a whole iceberg leaf and place 2 tablespoons of pork in the centre, carefully roll up the leaf and eat like a burrito.

SPICY WOK-BRAISED RICE CAKES

As an alternative to my favourite doubanjiang chilli bean paste, let me introduce you to its sweeter Korean counterpart, gochujang, equally pungent with that unmistakable fermented aroma, yet a little more subtle in flavour.

Prep 10 minutes
Cook 18 minutes
Serves 2

Equipment
Wok

500g (1lb 2oz) hot pot rice cakes
750ml (3 cups) fish stock
2 tbsp sugar
2 tbsp fish sauce
1 tbsp light soy sauce
3 tbsp gochujang
5 spring onions (scallions), cut into
    5cm (2in) lengths, whites and
    greens separated
2 tsp chilli (red pepper) flakes
2 garlic cloves, minced
175g (6oz) fishcake or fish balls,
    sliced
200g (7oz) Chinese leaf
    (Napa cabbage), cut into
    bite-sized pieces

Begin by loosening the rice cakes in warm water, following the packet instructions.

Add the fish stock, sugar, fish sauce, soy sauce, gochujang paste, spring onion (scallion) whites, chilli (red pepper) flakes and garlic to a wok and gently bring to a simmer, stirring to ensure the sugar has dissolved and the ingredients are well combined. Add the soaked rice cakes and cook for 8–10 minutes until tender, then add the fishcake and cook for a further 2–3 minutes. Finally, add the Chinese leaf (Napa cabbage) and spring onion greens and cook for a further 2 minutes. Check for seasoning and, if required, add a little more gochujang paste or fish sauce to your liking. Transfer to deep serving bowls and tuck in – this is best served hot.

CHINESE-STYLE MACARONI SOUP

Popular in the street food cafés of Hong Kong and classically topped with Spam and a fried egg, this soup is the epitome of simple comfort food.

Prep 10 minutes
Cook 20 minutes
Serves 2

Equipment
Large saucepan

2 tsp vegetable oil or use spray oil
2 celery sticks, cut into bite-sized
  pieces
1 onion, sliced
thumb-sized piece of ginger,
  peeled and cut into matchsticks
2 garlic cloves, crushed
  but left whole
3 spring onions (scallions),
  whites cut into 5cm (2in) lengths
  and greens sliced
2 litres (8 cups) water
2 tbsp chicken powder
  (for vegetarian option,
  use vegetable stock)
2 tbsp light soy sauce
200g (7oz) macaroni
1 tsp sesame oil
salt and white pepper, to taste

For the toppings
Pick and choose any or all of the
  following topping ingredients,
  or simply leave them out:
1 cooked chicken breast, shredded
350g (12oz) cooked seafood
150g (5oz) chopped ham
120g (1 cup) peas
8 mushrooms of your choice,
  thinly sliced
150g (5oz) marinated tofu pieces

Place a 3–4-litre (13¼–17½-cup) saucepan over a medium-low heat, add the oil along with the celery and onion and fry gently until softened. Next, add the ginger, garlic and spring onion whites and continue to fry until fragrant. (Do not have your heat too high as this will caramelize the ingredients and leave you with black specks in your soup.)

Now add the water along with the chicken powder and light soy sauce and turn up the heat a little. Once the soup is boiling, add the macaroni, reduce the heat to a simmer, cover and cook for 10 minutes. Now add any of your toppings and continue to cook gently for a further 5 minutes or until the macaroni is tender and the topping ingredients are hot. Taste and adjust the seasoning to your liking with white pepper and salt. Transfer to serving bowls and then sprinkle with the chopped spring onion greens and the sesame oil.

CHINESE-STYLE OXTAIL SOUP

Big on flavour but light on the body, this typical soup is deliciously nourishing and packed with healthy vegetables.

Prep 30 minutes
Cook 2 hours 45 minutes
Serves 3–4

Equipment
Casserole

12 dried shiitake (poku) mushrooms
1 tbsp vegetable oil
450–500g (1lb–1lb 2oz) oxtail, cut into bite-sized chunks
125ml (½ cup) Chinese rice wine (Shaoxing wine)
3 litres (12 cups) beef stock
2 tbsp fish sauce
1 tbsp brown sugar
thumb-sized piece of ginger, peeled and cut into matchsticks
5 red bird's-eye chillies, roughly chopped into pieces
80g (½ cup) raw peanuts
350g (12oz) mooli (daikon), cut into bite-sized pieces
150g (5oz) carrots, peeled and cut into bite-sized pieces
200g (7oz) bok choy, cut into bite-sized pieces
salt and white pepper, to taste

Place the shiitake (poku) mushrooms in a bowl and pour over boiling water to rehydrate, leaving them to steep for 20–30 minutes. Drain, remove the tough stalks and then chop into bite-sized pieces.

Place a medium-large flameproof casserole over a medium-high heat, add the oil and, once hot, add the oxtail and brown on all sides; this will take about 8–10 minutes. Next, add the Chinese rice wine and deglaze the bottom of the pot. Once the wine has begun to reduce, you can add the beef stock, fish sauce, brown sugar, ginger, mushrooms, chillies and peanuts. Bring to the boil and skim off any foam that accumulates on the surface. Once the foam has been removed, turn the heat down to a low simmer, cover and cook for 2 hours.

After 2 hours, add the mooli (daikon) and carrot and continue to cook for a further 20 minutes with the lid on. Once the mooli is tender, bring the soup back to the boil and add the bok choy, then reduce the heat and simmer for a final 5 minutes. Taste and adjust the seasoning with salt and pepper if required.

WATERCRESS AND GINGER SOUP WITH MEATBALLS

Rich in vitamins and antioxidants and full of peppery warmth, this light yet hearty broth with lightly seasoned pork balls is the perfect fix for your mind, body and soul.

Prep 10 minutes
Cook 12 minutes
Serves 2

Equipment
Large saucepan
Food processor

2 litres (8 cups) water
palm-sized piece of ginger, peeled and sliced
1½ tbsp chicken powder
2 tbsp light soy sauce
300g (10½oz) fresh watercress
pinch of white pepper
salt, to taste
1 tsp sesame oil

For the meatballs
350g (12oz) minced (ground) pork
1 spring onion (scallion), finely chopped
1 tbsp minced ginger
1 tbsp Chinese rice wine (Shaoxing wine)
2 tbsp light soy sauce
pinch of white pepper
½ tsp chicken powder
¼ tsp sugar
1 egg white
1 tsp cornflour (cornstarch)
vegetable oil, for greasing your hands

Place all of the meatball ingredients into a food processor and mix on medium speed for at least 6 minutes until the mixture becomes thick and sticky. Now lightly coat your hands in oil and form ping-pong-sized balls with the mixture. Place on a plate to one side ready for cooking.

In a 3–4-litre (13¼–17½-cup) saucepan, add the water, ginger, chicken powder and soy sauce and bring to the boil, then add the meatballs and bring the soup back to the boil before reducing the heat to a simmer. Cook over a low heat for 8 minutes, using a spoon to skim off any froth during cooking. Once the meatballs are cooked all the way through, add the watercress. Once wilted, add the white pepper, taste and adjust the seasoning with salt if required. Finally, turn off the heat, drizzle with the sesame oil and serve warm.

SEAWEED RICE WRAPS

Sushi made simple! Arrange a plateful to serve or enjoy as a 'build your own' sharing platter.

Prep 10 minutes
Cook 30 minutes, plus 15 minutes
   cooling
Serves 2–3

Equipment
Saucepan

½ cucumber, cut into matchsticks
½ red (bell) pepper, deseeded and
   cut into matchsticks
100g (3½oz) smoked salmon
145g (5¼oz) tuna mixed with 2 tbsp
   mayonnaise
1 avocado, sliced
3 tbsp mayonnaise, for spreading
2 tbsp wasabi, for smearing
50g (1¾oz) pickled ginger
6 nori sheets, cut in half
3 tbsp light soy sauce, for dipping

For the rice
500g (1lb 2oz) sushi rice
2 tbsp sugar
½ tsp salt
60ml (¼ cup) white rice vinegar

Place the rice in a saucepan and wash three times in lukewarm water, then add enough water so it covers the rice approximately 2cm (¾in) above the surface. Place over a medium-high heat and, once boiling, turn down to a simmer, cover with a lid and leave to cook for 10 minutes. After 10 minutes turn off the heat and leave to steam for 15 minutes. Do not remove the lid until the end of the steaming time.

Dissolve the sugar and salt in the vinegar.

Empty the cooked rice into a large bowl, add the vinegar, salt and sugar mixture and fold together. You ideally want to keep folding for at least 3–5 minutes to ensure the vinegar is evenly distributed through the rice. Allow to cool.

Place the remaining ingredients on to serving plates or into bowls.

To build a wrap, take a piece of nori and carefully spread a single layer of rice across the entire surface, add your fillings to one half, then fold the other half over the top. Dip in the soy sauce and enjoy.

Kwoklyn's tip
When adding the water to the rice for cooking, if you level the rice in the pan and gently touch your middle finger to the top of the rice, the water should just reach your first knuckle. Of course, everyone's hands are different, but this is a great trick that very rarely falls short of a good measure, so give it a try!

OVEN-ROASTED CAPITAL SHORT RIBS

Melt-in-the-mouth meaty short ribs roasted to the point of falling off the bone and then smothered in sweet Capital sauce... Need I say more?!

Prep 5 minutes
Cook 3 hours 20 minutes
Serves 3–4

Equipment
Casserole

1.8kg (4lb) bone-in beef ribs, cut into 5–7.5cm (2–3in) pieces (your butcher should be able to chop these for you)
pinch of salt
pinch of black pepper

For the sauce
1 tbsp oyster sauce
6 tbsp tomato ketchup
3 tbsp brown sauce
1 tbsp Worcestershire sauce
2 tbsp sugar
60ml (¼ cup) chicken stock
pinch of white pepper

Preheat the oven to 140°C (275°F).

Season the ribs with the salt and black pepper, place in a medium flameproof casserole and roast in the oven for 3 hours, turning every hour. Once the meat has started to fall off the bone, carefully pour off any cooking liquid.

Combine all the sauce ingredients in a bowl and pour over the ribs, giving them a quick toss to coat, and then place back in the oven for a further 20 minutes. Once the glaze is sticky, remove from the oven and serve.

CHAR SIU PORK PASTIES

My take on a dim sum favourite, Char Siu Sou, a juicy sweet pork filling encased in flaky puff pastry and scattered with nutty sesame seeds. Perfect as a starter, snack on the go or lunchbox treat.

Prep 20 minutes
Cook 30 minutes, plus 10 minutes
  cooling
Serves 2–3

Equipment
Baking sheet

3 sheets of ready-rolled puff pastry
  (approx. 980g/2lb 3oz)
2 eggs, beaten
2 tbsp sesame seeds

For the filling
450g (1lb) minced (ground) pork
1 bunch of spring onions (scallions),
  finely chopped
2 garlic cloves, minced
1 tsp grated ginger
5 tbsp hoisin sauce
3 tbsp yellow bean sauce
2 tbsp sugar
1 tbsp Chinese rice wine
  (Shaoxing wine)
1 tsp Chinese five spice

Preheat the oven to 200°C (400°F).

Place all the filling ingredients in a bowl, mix thoroughly to combine and then divide into 6 equal portions.

Cut each sheet of pastry in half widthways, then fill one side of each new rectangle of pastry with filling, ensuring you leave enough room around the edge to seal. Lightly brush the edges with beaten egg and then fold the empty half of each rectangle over the filling to create a triangle. Gently press the edges together to seal, then use a fork to crimp the edges. Once all of your pasties have been made, brush with egg and then sprinkle with the sesame seeds.

Place the assembled pasties on a non-stick baking sheet and then into your hot oven to bake for 25–30 minutes or until golden brown and the filling is completely cooked. Allow to cool for 10 minutes before serving.

BLACK PEPPER AND FIVE SPICE WINGS

Though not the meatiest part of the chicken, the wings are very popular in China as they offer more taste and texture than breast meat, plus they are so inexpensive you can make a huge batch to tuck in to.

Prep 5 minutes
Cook 40 minutes
Serves 4

Equipment
Casserole or wok

900g (2lb) chicken wings
1 tbsp ground black pepper
1 tbsp Chinese five spice
5 tbsp dark soy sauce
2 spring onions (scallions), finely sliced

In a large bowl, mix all the ingredients together (except the spring onions/scallions) and thoroughly coat the chicken wings. Place the wings bottom up in a flameproof casserole or wok in a single layer, covering the base of the pot completely, and pour over any remaining marinade.

Place the lid on your casserole or wok and cook over a low heat for 20 minutes before turning the wings and repeating the process. If all the liquid has evaporated, pour over a small amount of water, as the wings will need a further 20 minutes (40 minutes in total).

Place the cooked wings on a serving dish, pour over the cooking juices and serve garnished with the sliced spring onions.

RICE

CHINESE SAUSAGE FRIED RICE

Chinese sausage (lap cheong) carries a very distinct smoky sweetness with an underlying hint of Chinese rice wine, perfect for ramping up the flavour in this simple fried rice.

Prep 5 minutes
Cook 8 minutes
Serves 2

Equipment
Wok

2 tbsp vegetable oil
2 eggs, beaten
3 Chinese sausages (lap cheong),
    thinly sliced
1 onion, diced
3 spring onions (scallions),
    finely sliced
500g (1lb 2oz) cooked rice, chilled
    (you can use long grain or
    basmati)
60g (½ cup) peas
2 tsp light soy sauce
1 tsp dark soy sauce
1½ tbsp oyster sauce
pinch of white pepper
salt, to taste
2 tsp sesame oil

Place a wok over a medium-high heat, add the oil and, once smoking, add the beaten eggs. Once the egg is set, stir it lightly to break it up, add the sliced sausages and cook for a further 2 minutes. Next, add the onion and spring onions (scallions) and, once these have seared, add the rice. Continue to fry the rice for 2–3 minutes – you want the grains to lightly toast, which will give your dish a slightly nutty flavour. Once the rice is heated all the way through, add the peas followed by the light and dark soy sauces, oyster sauce and white pepper. Mix thoroughly and taste. At this point you can add salt if required. Once you are happy with the seasoning, turn off the heat and drizzle with the sesame oil.

Transfer to serving bowls and enjoy.

BREAKFAST FRIED RICE

Rice is a staple in most households in China and I've been known to start many a day with a bowl of quick fried rice, stacked out with a selection of meaty morsels, and topped with a fried egg cooked to crispy perfection while retaining that creamy yolk for dribbling through the rice. Top it with a generous dollop of my favourite sweet chilli sauce and I'm good to go!

Prep 5 minutes
Cook 15 minutes
Serves 2

Equipment
Wok

4 eggs
3 tbsp vegetable oil
200g (7oz) pancetta, cut into cubes
1 small onion, finely diced
2 garlic cloves, minced
150g (5oz) diced cooked smoked
   sausage or pepperoni
150g (5oz) diced Spam
3 spring onions (scallions),
   finely sliced
500g (1lb 2oz) cooked rice, chilled
   (you can use long grain or
   basmati)
1 tbsp light soy sauce
2 tsp dark soy sauce
pinch of white pepper
salt, to taste
2 tsp sesame oil

Beat two of the eggs and set to one side.

Place a wok over a medium-high heat, add 1 tablespoon of the oil and, once smoking, add the pancetta and fry until golden, then add the beaten eggs and allow to set. Once your egg is cooked, stir it lightly to break it up, then add the onion, garlic, cubed sausage and Spam and cook for a further 2 minutes. Next, add the spring onions (scallions) and, once these have seared, add the rice. Continue to fry the rice for 2–3 minutes – you want the grains to lightly toast, which will give your dish a slightly nutty flavour. Once the rice is heated all the way through, add the light and dark soy sauces and white pepper. Mix thoroughly and taste. At this point you can add salt if required. Once you are happy with the seasoning, turn off the heat, drizzle with the sesame oil and transfer to your serving bowls.

Place the wok back over a high heat and add the remaining 2 tablespoons of oil. Once smoking, carefully crack the remaining 2 eggs into the oil and fry until they have a crispy bottom. Flip the eggs over and then immediately place on top of your rice.

Transfer to serving bowls and tuck in.

YEUNG CHOW (YANGZHOU) RICE

Often called 'House' or 'Special Fried Rice' on your local Chinese takeaway or restaurant menu, story has it that the name actually comes from the city of Yangzhou where sailors were said to have added scraps from their lunch into fried rice for dinner.

Prep 5 minutes
Cook 10 minutes
Serves 2

Equipment
Wok

2 tbsp vegetable oil
100g (3½oz) pancetta,
   cut into cubes (or you can
   use cooked char siu pork)
2 eggs, beaten
150g (5oz) cooked chicken,
   cut into cubes
60g (½ cup) cooked prawns (shrimp)
3 spring onions (scallions),
   finely sliced
250g (9oz) cooked rice, chilled (you
   can use long grain or basmati)
100g (3½oz) mixed frozen
   vegetables, defrosted
1 tbsp light soy sauce
2 tsp dark soy sauce
1½ tbsp oyster sauce
pinch of white pepper
salt, to taste
2 tsp sesame oil

Place a wok over a medium-high heat, add the oil and, once smoking, add the pancetta and fry until golden. Then add the beaten eggs and allow to set in the wok. Once the egg is cooked, stir it lightly to break it up, then add the chicken and prawns (shrimp) and cook for a further 2 minutes. Next, add the spring onions (scallions) and, once these have seared, add the rice and give everything a good mix. Continue to fry the rice for 2–3 minutes – you want the grains to lightly toast, which will give the dish a slightly nutty flavour. Once the rice is heated all the way through, add the mixed vegetables followed by the light and dark soy sauces, oyster sauce and white pepper. Mix thoroughly and give your rice a taste. At this point you can add salt if required. Once you are happy with the seasoning, turn off the heat and drizzle with the sesame oil.

Transfer to serving bowls and enjoy.

CHICKEN AND SHIITAKE POT RICE

Juicy marinated chicken and earthy mushrooms steamed atop delicate, fragrant Thai rice; for me this is perfect comfort food. And don't be afraid of the rice catching on the bottom of the pot – trust me, it's the best part!

Prep 35 minutes
Marinate 20 minutes +
Cook 40 minutes
Serves 2

Equipment
Clay pot or large saucepan

300g (10½oz) skinless, boneless chicken thighs, cut into bite-sized pieces
1 tsp salt
1 tbsp white rice vinegar
8 dried Chinese or shiitake (poku) mushrooms
3 pieces of dried wood ear mushroom (black fungus)
180g (1 cup) Thai fragrant rice (or long-grain rice)
250ml (1 cup) chicken stock
1 tbsp vegetable oil
2 slices of ginger
1 spring onion (scallion), finely sliced, whites and greens separated

For the marinade
½ tbsp Chinese rice wine (Shaoxing wine)
1 tbsp cornflour (cornstarch)
1 tbsp oyster sauce
1 tsp dark soy sauce
1 tbsp light soy sauce
1 tsp pure sesame oil (not blended)
pinch of sugar
pinch of salt
pinch of white pepper

Place the chicken in a bowl along with the salt and rice vinegar. Cover with water and massage the chicken with your hands for 30 seconds, then allow to sit for 30 minutes. This process will tenderize the chicken and remove any impurities. Drain and pat dry with kitchen paper.

While the chicken is tenderizing, place the dried mushrooms into a bowl and pour over boiling water. After 30 minutes, once the mushrooms have rehydrated, cut off the tough stalks and then slice into bite-sized pieces.

Place the drained chicken in a bowl along with the rehydrated mushrooms and all the marinade ingredients. Massage the marinade into the chicken, cover and set to one side to marinate for at least 20 minutes or ideally for 2 hours in the fridge.

Place the rice in a bowl and wash 2–3 times until the water becomes less cloudy, then cover with water and allow to soak for 35 minutes. Once soaked, pour off the excess water and place the rice into a 3–4-litre (13¼–17½-cup) clay pot or large saucepan. Pour over the chicken stock and oil, evenly spread the marinated chicken (along with any remaining marinade) and mushrooms over the top of the rice and then top with the sliced ginger and spring onion (scallion) whites. Place the pot over a medium heat and, once the liquid is bubbling and has begun to be absorbed, turn the heat down to its lowest setting, put on the lid and cook for 25 minutes. Turn off the heat and allow it to stand with the lid on for a further 10 minutes – no peeking! (If you like a crispy bottom to your rice, you can leave the heat on low for the last 10 minutes.) Check the chicken is cooked all the way through and then garnish with the spring onion greens and serve.

BLACK BEAN CHICKEN AND TOFU POT RICE

These salty, savoury, fermented black beans cook down amongst the chicken and tofu to impart their rich umami and lift this rice pot to another level.

Prep 35 minutes
Marinate 20 minutes +
Cook 40 minutes
Serves 2

Equipment
Clay pot or large saucepan

300g (10½oz) skinless, boneless
  chicken thighs, cut into bite-sized
  pieces
1 tsp salt
1 tbsp white rice vinegar
8 pieces of pre-fried tofu,
  cut into bite-sized pieces
  (available to buy from
  East Asian supermarkets)
1 spring onion (scallion), finely sliced,
  whites and greens separated
1 red bird's-eye chilli, deseeded and
  thinly sliced
180g (1 cup) Thai fragrant rice
  (or long-grain rice)

For the marinade
½ tbsp Chinese rice wine
  (Shaoxing wine)
1 tbsp oyster sauce
1 tsp dark soy sauce
1 tbsp light soy sauce
2 tbsp fermented black beans
1 tbsp vegetable oil
pinch of sugar
pinch of salt
pinch of white pepper

Place the chicken in a bowl along with the salt and rice vinegar. Cover with water and massage the chicken with your hands for 30 seconds, then allow to sit for 30 minutes. This process will tenderize the chicken and remove any impurities. Drain and pat dry with kitchen paper.

Now place the drained chicken in a clean bowl with the tofu, the spring onion (scallion) whites, chilli and all the marinade ingredients. Massage the marinade into the chicken, cover and set to one side to marinate for at least 20 minutes or ideally for 2 hours in the fridge.

Place the rice in a bowl and wash 2–3 times until the water becomes less cloudy, then cover with water and allow to soak for 35 minutes. Once soaked, pour off the excess water and place the rice into a 3–4-litre (13¼–17½-cup) clay pot or large saucepan. Pour over 250ml (1 cup) of water and then evenly spread the marinated chicken (along with any remaining marinade) and tofu over the top of the rice. Place over a medium heat and, once the liquid is bubbling and has begun to be absorbed, turn the heat down to its lowest setting, put on the lid and cook for 25 minutes. Turn off the heat and allow it to stand with the lid on for a further 10 minutes – no peeking! (If you like a crispy bottom to your rice, you can leave the heat on low for the last 10 minutes.) Check the chicken is cooked all the way through and then garnish with the spring onion greens and serve.

GARLIC CHICKEN POT RICE

Not only is this simple to prepare and keeps washing-up to a minimum, this one-pot winner allows the rice to take on all of the flavours of the marinade.

Prep 35 minutes
Marinate 20 minutes +
Cook 40 minutes
Serves 2

Equipment
Clay pot or large saucepan

350–400g (12–14oz) boneless,
  skinless chicken thighs, cut into
  bite-sized pieces
1 tsp salt
1 tbsp white rice vinegar
180g (1 cup) Thai fragrant rice
  (or long-grain rice)
2 spring onions (scallions),
  finely sliced

For the marinade
8 garlic gloves, minced
1 small onion, finely diced
½ green (bell) pepper, deseeded
  and finely diced
2 tbsp oyster sauce
2 tbsp Chinese rice wine
  (Shaoxing wine)
1 tsp sugar
1 tbsp light soy sauce
1 tsp dark soy sauce
1 tsp sesame oil
pinch of white pepper
1 tbsp vegetable oil

Place the chicken in a bowl along with the salt and rice vinegar. Cover with water and massage the chicken with your hands for 30 seconds, then allow to sit for 30 minutes. This process will tenderize the chicken and remove any impurities. Drain and pat dry with kitchen paper.

Place all the marinade ingredients in a bowl, add the drained chicken and use your hands to massage the marinade into the chicken. Cover and set to one side to marinate for at least 20 minutes or ideally for 2 hours in the fridge.

Place the rice in a bowl and wash 2–3 times until the water becomes less cloudy, then cover with water and allow to soak for 35 minutes. Once soaked, pour off the excess water and place the rice into a 3–4-litre (13¼–17½-cup) clay pot or large saucepan. Pour over 250ml (1 cup) of water and evenly spread over the marinated chicken (along with any remaining marinade) and top with half of the spring onions (scallions). Place over a medium heat and, once the water begins to bubble and has begun to be absorbed, turn the heat down to its lowest setting, put on the lid and allow to cook for 25 minutes. Turn off the heat and allow it to stand with the lid on for a further 10 minutes – no peeking! (If you like a crispy bottom to your rice, you can leave the heat on low for the last 10 minutes.) Check the chicken is cooked and then sprinkle with the remaining chopped spring onions and serve.

Kwoklyn's tip
If you like a good strong hit of garlic, mince the cloves finely before marinating the chicken. If you like a more subtle flavour, crush the cloves with the flat of your knife but leave them whole so that they can impart their flavour as they cook but you can still pick them out as you eat.

STEAMED PORK BELLY AND STICKY RICE

My oversized tweak to a dim sum favourite, belly pork sticky rice parcels. The fat on the marinated pork belly melts into the rice, creating a rich, sticky glaze, and the bamboo leaves add a refreshing earthy element to the dish.

Prep 20 minutes
Marinate 8 hours +
Cook 2 hours
Serves 2–3

Equipment
Bamboo steamer

300g (1½ cups) uncooked sticky rice
5 dried bamboo leaves
150g (5oz) pork belly, cut into
   bite-sized pieces
2 tbsp light soy sauce,
   plus extra to serve
1 tsp dark soy sauce
2 pinches of salt
pinch of white pepper
1 tsp sugar
2 tbsp Chinese rice wine
   (Shaoxing wine)
1 Chinese sausage (lap cheong),
   cut into 1cm (½in) dice
2 spring onions (scallions),
   thinly sliced
50g (1¾oz) dried shrimps

In separate bowls, soak the uncooked sticky rice and bamboo leaves for at least 8 hours or overnight if possible.

Place the pork in a bowl, add 1 tablespoon of the light soy sauce, the dark soy sauce, a pinch of salt, the white pepper, sugar and rice wine and mix well. Cover and marinate in the fridge for at least 8 hours or overnight.

After the soaking time, rinse each bamboo leaf with clean water. Drain the soaked sticky rice and mix in the remaining pinch of salt and the remaining 1 tablespoon of light soy sauce. Add the Chinese sausage (lap cheong), spring onions (scallions) and dried shrimps and mix well.

Line an 18cm (7in) bamboo steamer with the soaked bamboo leaves (retaining enough to cover the rice), then add half the rice mixture followed by a layer of marinated belly pork, followed with the remaining rice. Cover the rice with the remaining bamboo leaves and then place the lid on the bamboo steamer. Place the steamer over a pan of water and steam the rice for 2 hours.

At the end of cooking, peel back the leaves and check the pork is tender, then carefully remove the steamer basket from the pan of water and place in the centre of the table to serve.

Delicious served in small rice bowls with an additional drizzle of light soy sauce.

BLACK BEAN AND PORK RIB RICE

Clay-pot rice dishes have been cooked in China for more than 2,000 years, and a classic combination that should be on everyone's kitchen hit list is this Cantonese black bean pork ribs rice pot. The rice gets its rich flavour from the marinated ribs on the top, while the meat should slide off the bone after time well spent on the marinating and tenderizing processes.

Prep 35 minutes
Marinate 2 hours +
Cook 40 minutes
Serves 2

Equipment
Clay pot or large saucepan

350–400g (12–14oz) pork ribs,
  cut into 2.5cm (1in) pieces
1 tsp salt
1 tbsp white rice vinegar
180g (1 cup) Thai fragrant rice
  (or long-grain rice)
1 red bird's-eye chilli, deseeded
  and finely sliced
2 spring onions (scallions),
  finely sliced

For the marinade
2 tbsp fermented black beans
3 garlic cloves, minced
1 tbsp oyster sauce
1 tbsp Chinese rice wine
  (Shaoxing wine)
1 tsp sugar
1 tbsp light soy sauce
1 tsp dark soy sauce
pinch of white pepper
1 tbsp vegetable oil

Place the ribs in a bowl, add the salt and rice vinegar and then cover with water. Allow to soak for 30 minutes. This process will help remove any impurities from the meat and help loosen the muscle fibres, ensuring a tender rib.

Once the ribs have soaked, drain and place on kitchen paper to absorb any excess water. Place all the marinade ingredients in a bowl, add the drained ribs and, using your hands, massage the marinade into the ribs. Cover and set to one side to marinate for at least 2 hours, or overnight in the fridge if possible.

Place the rice in a bowl and wash 2–3 times until the water becomes less cloudy, then cover with water and allow to soak for 35 minutes. Once soaked, pour off the excess water and place the rice into a 3–4-litre (13¼–17½-cup) clay pot or saucepan. Pour over 250ml (1 cup) of water and evenly spread over the marinated pork ribs, then sprinkle with the chilli and half of the spring onions (scallions). Place over a medium heat and, once the water begins to bubble and has begun to be absorbed, turn the heat down to its lowest setting, put on the lid and allow to cook for 25 minutes. Turn off the heat and allow it to stand with the lid on for a further 10 minutes – no peeking! (If you like a crispy bottom to your rice, you can leave the heat on low for the last 10 minutes.) Check the ribs are cooked, sprinkle with the remaining spring onions and serve.

NOODLES

CREAMY SPICY KOREAN UDON

A quick dish to end those weeknight meal dilemmas – springy, slurpy udon smothered in crispy garlicky bacon shards, crunchy beansprouts and a sumptuously Korean-style sauce.

Prep 10 minutes
Cook 8 minutes
Serves 2

Equipment
Wok

2 nests straight-to-wok udon
  noodles
200g (7oz) streaky bacon,
  cut into 2cm (¾in) pieces
1 large onion, sliced
3 garlic cloves, minced
3 spring onions (scallions),
  roughly chopped
2 tbsp gochujang chilli paste
1½ tbsp light soy sauce
125ml (½ cup) single (light) cream
100g (3½oz) beansprouts

Place the noodle nests in a colander or sieve (strainer) and loosen under hot water. Drain and set to one side.

Heat a wok over a medium-high heat, add the chopped bacon and fry until golden brown, then add the onion and garlic and cook until the onion becomes translucent. Add the spring onions (scallions), gochujang paste and soy sauce, mix well and then add the cream followed by the beansprouts and gently stir to combine. Once heated all the way through, stir in the drained noodles and serve.

CRISPY FRIED GARLIC NOODLES

Deliciously fragrant and quite literally oozing with garlicky goodness. A dish to be shared with a 'very close' loved one... maybe not first date material!

Prep 10 minutes
Cook 8 minutes
Serves 2

Equipment
Wok

150–200g (5–7oz) straight-to-wok noodles of your choice
60ml (¼ cup) water
3 tbsp light soy sauce
1 tbsp dark soy sauce
1 tbsp oyster sauce
1 tbsp Chinese rice wine (Shaoxing wine)
2 tbsp vegetable oil
2 tbsp salted butter
1 bulb of garlic, around 12 cloves, peeled and roughly chopped
1 onion, finely diced
½ thumb-sized piece of ginger, peeled and cut into matchsticks
3 spring onions (scallions), whites cut into 5cm (2in) lengths and greens finely chopped

Place the noodles in a colander or sieve (strainer) and loosen under hot water. Drain and set to one side.

In a bowl mix together the water, light and dark soy sauces, oyster sauce and rice wine.

Place a wok over a medium-low heat, add the oil and butter, followed by the chopped garlic and fry for 1–2 minutes until fragrant. Turn the heat up to medium-high and continue to cook the garlic until it begins to brown and go crispy (being very careful not to let it burn). Once browned, transfer to a bowl.

To the residual oil, add the onion, ginger and spring onion (scallion) whites, fry until softened and then add the noodles. Fry for a further minute and then add the sauce mixture, stirring to combine. Once everything is piping hot, turn off the heat and add the cooked garlic. Give everything a good mix, transfer to a serving plate and top with the spring onion greens.

KING PRAWN PAD THAI

A popular street food dish originating from Thailand, the flat rice noodles are tossed in the classic Thai flavours of fish sauce, tamarind paste, lime juice and chilli sauce. Spicy, tangy and sweet, all in one mouthful.

Prep 5 minutes
Cook 8 minutes
Serves 2–3

Equipment
Wok

350g (12oz) straight-to-wok thick rice noodles
3 tbsp vegetable oil
3 eggs, beaten
350g (12oz) raw king prawns (jumbo shrimp), shelled and deveined
1 onion, finely diced
3 spring onions (scallions), cut into 5cm (2in) lengths
200g (4 cups) beansprouts

For the sauce
2 tbsp fish sauce
2 tbsp light soy sauce
2 tbsp white rice vinegar
2 tbsp lime juice
2 tbsp brown sauce
2 tbsp Sriracha chilli sauce
1 tbsp tamarind paste
2 tbsp brown sugar

Place the noodles in a colander or sieve (strainer) and loosen under hot water. Drain and set to one side.

In a bowl, mix together all the sauce ingredients.

Place a wok over a medium-high heat, add 1 tablespoon of the oil and, once smoking, add the beaten eggs. Mix gently to break up and, once cooked, transfer to a plate and set to one side.

Add another tablespoon of oil to the wok and, once hot, add the king prawns (jumbo shrimp). Once they have turned pink and are slightly charred, transfer to the plate with the eggs. Add the remaining tablespoon of oil and fry the onion until golden brown. Now add the spring onions (scallions), fry for a further 1–2 minutes and then add the sauce mixture along with the noodles, beansprouts, king prawns and egg. Stir to ensure the ingredients are well combined and continue to cook until everything is hot. Serve immediately.

Perfect served with a wedge of fresh lime.

RED CURRY RAMEN

Super quick and tasty, impress your lunch partner with a bowl of noodles in a spicy red curry coconut broth; or just serve yourself a hearty bowl, cheerful in the knowledge that you've got a second helping waiting in the wings!

Prep 5 minutes
Cook 8 minutes
Serves 2

Equipment
Large saucepan

250g (9oz) pork loin, thinly sliced
2 nests dried ramen noodles
2 spring onions (scallions),
   thinly sliced

For the broth
400ml (14fl oz) can coconut milk
2 lemongrass stalks, bruised
2 shallots, sliced
3 tbsp Thai red curry paste
thumb-sized piece of ginger,
   peeled and sliced
1 tbsp tomato purée (paste)
3 garlic cloves, minced
1 litre (4 cups) water
1 tbsp chicken powder
6 makrut lime leaves
2 tbsp fish sauce (or light soy sauce
   if preferred)

Place all the broth ingredients in a 3–4-litre (13¼–17½-cup) saucepan over a medium-high heat and bring to the boil. Then add the sliced pork, turn down to a simmer and cook for a further 5 minutes. Finally, add the ramen noodles to the pan and, once the noodles have softened, transfer to a serving bowl and garnish with the spring onions (scallions).

Kwoklyn's tip
Finish with a couple of halved soft-boiled eggs and you're in ramen bowl heaven.

DRUNKEN CHICKEN NOODLES

Contrary to what the name would suggest, the chicken in this noodle dish is not drenched in alcohol; a common theory behind the Thai name (Pad Kee Mao) is that they are simply a perfect recovery dish for the day after the night before...

Prep 10 minutes
Cook 25 minutes
Serves 2

Equipment
Wok

400g (14oz) fresh flat rice noodles (ho fun)
2 tbsp vegetable oil
350g (12oz) boneless skin-on chicken thighs, cut into 2.5cm (1in) pieces
2 garlic cloves, minced
thumb-sized piece of ginger, peeled and sliced
3 spring onions (scallions), cut into 5cm (2in) lengths, whites and greens separated
300g (10oz) choy sum, cut into 5cm (2in) lengths, stalks and leaves separated
3 tbsp oyster sauce
2 tbsp light soy sauce
1 tbsp dark soy sauce
2 tsp chicken powder
125ml (½ cup) red wine
1 tbsp cornflour (cornstarch) mixed with 2 tbsp water
1 tsp sesame oil

Place the noodles in a colander or sieve (strainer) and loosen under hot water, drain and set to one side.

Heat a wok with the oil over a medium-high heat, then add the chicken thighs and cook for about 12–18 minutes, turning occasionally until golden brown and cooked through. Now add the garlic and ginger and fry until fragrant, then add the spring onion (scallion) whites and choy sum stalks along with the oyster sauce, light and dark soy sauces, chicken powder and red wine. Bring to the boil, then add the softened noodles, spring onion greens and choy sum leaves and combine. Give the cornflour (cornstarch) mixture a stir and pour into the noodle sauce, mixing continuously until the sauce reaches your desired consistency. Turn off the heat and drizzle with the sesame oil.

BRAISED CHICKEN WITH GLASS NOODLES

Similar to the Korean *Jjimdak*, a dish that is thought to have originated from the city of Andong in the 1970s and 80s, the braised chicken and soft glass noodles in this dish soak up the spicy sweet soy-based sauce, giving you full flavour with every mouthful.

Prep 30 minutes
Cook 30 minutes
Serves 2

Equipment
Casserole

3 dried Chinese mushrooms, sliced
200g (7oz) glass (mung bean) noodles
450g (1lb) boneless, skinless chicken thighs, cut into bite-sized pieces
1 tsp salt
1 tbsp white rice vinegar
2 large carrots, peeled and cut into 3cm (1¼in) cubes
3 spring onions (scallions), whites chopped into 5cm (2in) lengths, greens cut into rings
8 shallots, peeled and halved
2 whole red chillies, chopped into 2cm (¾in) pieces
1 tbsp sesame oil
1 tbsp toasted sesame seeds

For the sauce
1 litre (4 cups) water
2 garlic cloves, minced
1 tbsp ginger paste
3 tbsp oyster sauce
80ml (⅓ cup) light soy sauce
2 tbsp Chinese rice wine (Shaoxing wine)
1 tbsp white rice vinegar
3 tbsp honey
pinch of white pepper

Begin by placing the dried mushrooms in a bowl and soaking them in boiling water for around 30 minutes to rehydrate. Drain, cut into slices and set to one side.

In another bowl, place the dried glass noodles and soak them in warm water for 10 minutes until soft. Drain and set to one side.

Next, place the chicken thighs in a bowl, add the salt and white rice vinegar. Cover with water and allow to soak for 30 minutes. This process will help to remove any impurities from the chicken and loosen the muscle fibres. Drain and set to one side.

Place the drained chicken and all the sauce ingredients into a 3–4-litre (13¼–17½-cup) casserole, bring to the boil and then turn down to a simmer, placing on the lid and allowing to cook for 5 minutes. Next add the carrots, Chinese mushrooms, spring onion (scallion) whites, shallots and red chillies, bring back to the boil, then turn down to a simmer, cover and cook for a further 15 minutes. Remove the lid and stir in the softened glass noodles, then continue to cook for another minute. Turn off the heat, drizzle with the sesame oil and garnish with toasted sesame seeds and spring onion greens.

CHILLI BEAN HOT POT-STYLE NOODLES

Chinese hot pots are traditionally served in the centre of the table; diners can then add their choice of meat, fish, tofu and veggies to the simmering pot of soup for quick cooking, before retrieving with a small wire ladle and topping with a selection of dipping sauces. This vegan version gives you all the flavour of a classic hot pot served simply with flat rice noodles.

Prep 5 minutes
Cook 8 minutes
Serves 2

Equipment
Large saucepan

2 tbsp vegetable oil
200g (4 cups) beansprouts
200g (7oz) choy sum or spinach,
   cut into bite-sized pieces
150g (5oz) bok choy, cut
   into bite-sized pieces
350g (12oz) thick rice noodles
1 spring onion (scallion),
   finely chopped

For the sauce
1 garlic clove, minced
1 tsp Chinese chilli oil
1 tbsp light soy sauce
½ tbsp white rice vinegar
1½ tbsp doubanjiang (fermented
   chilli bean paste)
1 tsp sesame oil

Combine all the sauce ingredients together in a bowl and set to one side.

Heat a 2–3-litre (8¾–13¼-cup) saucepan of water over a medium-high heat and, once boiling, add the vegetable oil along with the beansprouts, choy sum and bok choy. After 1 minute of cooking, remove the veggies from the water and allow to drain. Add the noodles to the boiling water and cook until tender. Drain and transfer to your serving bowl. Now add the cooked veggies and sauce to the noodles and toss everything together. Finally, garnish with the chopped spring onion (scallion) and serve.

BEEF BRISKET NOODLE BOWL

A warming bowl of soup is sometimes all you need, so imagine how satisfying this dish will taste when topped with succulent beef and soft rice noodles.

Prep 5 minutes
Cook 1 hour 10 minutes
Serves 2

Equipment
Large saucepan

250g (9oz) beef brisket,
  cut into bite-sized chunks
1 tbsp vegetable oil
2 garlic cloves, sliced
3cm (1¼in) piece of ginger, peeled
  and sliced
3 spring onions (scallions), roughly
  chopped, whites and greens
  separated
¼ tsp Sichuan peppercorns, crushed
1 tbsp light soy sauce
1 tsp dark soy sauce
3 tbsp oyster sauce
1½ tbsp chicken powder
2 litres (8 cups) water
350–400g (12–14oz) fresh thick rice
  noodles (ho fun)
150g (5oz) Chinese leaf
  (Napa cabbage), sliced
  into bite-sized pieces
1 tsp sesame oil
salt and white pepper

Bring a large saucepan of water to the boil, add the beef and cook for 3 minutes, then drain and rinse under cold water and set to one side. This will help remove any impurities in the meat.

Wipe clean the same large saucepan and place over a medium heat, pour in the oil, then add the garlic, ginger and spring onion (scallion) whites and fry for 1 minute until fragrant. Add the drained beef brisket and Sichuan peppercorns and fry for 4 minutes until the beef has browned. Add the light and dark soy sauces, oyster sauce and chicken powder and continue frying for another minute. Add the water, bring to a low simmer and cook for 1 hour. Skim the top of the soup during cooking to remove any froth that has gathered.

Carefully loosen the strands of noodles under warm water and drain. Bring the soup back up to the boil and add the loosened noodles along with the Chinese leaf (Napa cabbage). Cook for 1–2 minutes, then turn off the heat, taste and adjust the seasoning to your preference with salt and white pepper. Add the sesame oil to the beef soup and transfer to your serving bowls. Top with the spring onion greens and serve hot.

Kwoklyn's tip
Fresh, thick rice noodles (ho fun) can be found in the fridge section of your local Chinese supermarket. If you cannot find the fresh noodles, you can use dried, but you will need to rehydrate before adding to the dish (following the instructions on the packet).

SPICY GROUND PORK UDON

Quick and easy with no heavy prep required, as everything just gets thrown straight into the wok, these plump spicy noodles are a simple midweek winner.

Prep 5 minutes
Cook 10 minutes
Serves 2

Equipment
Wok

1 tbsp vegetable oil
350g (12oz) minced (ground) pork
1 tbsp minced garlic
1 tbsp minced ginger
2 tbsp doubanjiang (fermented chilli bean paste)
2 tbsp honey
1 tbsp white rice vinegar
1 tbsp light soy sauce
2 tsp dark soy sauce
2 tsp chicken powder
1 cup (250ml) water
3 spring onions (scallions), roughly chopped into 5cm (2in) lengths
150g (5oz) bok choy, cut into bite-sized pieces
300g (10oz) straight-to-wok udon noodles
1 tbsp Chinese chilli oil

Place a wok over a medium-high heat, add the oil and then the pork and fry for 2–3 minutes or until slightly golden brown. Add the minced garlic and ginger and continue to fry until fragrant. Stir through the doubanjiang, along with the honey, vinegar, light and dark soy sauces, chicken powder and water, and bring to the boil. Once all of the ingredients are well combined and hot, turn down to a simmer and add the spring onions (scallions) and bok choy. Continue to cook for 2 minutes, then add the noodles and chilli oil and gently toss to combine the ingredients. Transfer to serving bowls and enjoy.

RED-COOKED BEEF WITH THICK RICE NOODLES

Perfect for tougher cuts of beef like brisket or chuck steak, red cooking is a classic Chinese braising technique using soy sauce, rice wine and sugar to achieve a deep red, thick caramelized sauce and melt-in-the-mouth meaty morsels. Tossed with thick rice noodles, this is one dish that will have the whole family drooling without breaking the budget.

Prep 5 minutes
Cook 3 hours 10 minutes
Serves 4

Equipment
Casserole

900g (2lb) beef, cut into bite-sized pieces (use chuck or brisket)
pinch of salt
1 tbsp vegetable oil
250ml (1 cup) light soy sauce
250ml (1 cup) Chinese rice wine (Shaoxing wine)
4 tbsp brown sugar
3cm (1¼in) piece of ginger, peeled and smashed
4 garlic cloves, crushed
2cm (¾in) piece of dried orange peel, broken into small pieces
2 star anise
1 tbsp chilli (red pepper) flakes
900ml (3½ cups) water
6 spring onions (scallions), whites cut into 5cm (2in) lengths, greens finely chopped
2 nests or 350–500g (12oz–1lb 2oz) fresh thick rice noodles (ho fun)

Place the beef in a large bowl and add the salt, then massage thoroughly into the meat. Heat a 3–4-litre (13¼–17½-cup) flameproof casserole over a medium heat with the oil, then add the salted beef and brown on all sides; this should take about 4 minutes. Add the remaining ingredients (except the spring onion/scallion greens and rice noodles), mix thoroughly and bring to the boil, then turn the heat down to low and cook for 2½ hours. Turn off the heat and allow the pot to stand for 30 minutes.

Carefully loosen the strands of noodles under warm water and drain. Bring the beef back up to the boil and, once hot, turn down to a simmer and add the loosened noodles. Add a little more water if the sauce has dried out during cooking and allow the noodles to gently soften and warm with the beef. Transfer to serving bowls and sprinkle with the spring onion greens.

Kwoklyn's tip
Fresh, thick rice noodles (ho fun) can be found in the fridge section of your local Chinese supermarket. If you cannot find the fresh noodles, you can use dried, but you will need to rehydrate before adding to the dish (following the instructions on the packet).

HOT BEEF STEW NOODLES

For a dish so seemingly simple to cook, prepare to be overwhelmed by the complexity of the flavours you're about to enjoy: tender meaty brisket shards, spicy sweet gochujang paste, salty fish sauce, and all balanced out by the crisp vegetables and springy glass (mung bean) noodles.

Prep 10 minutes
Marinate 20 minutes
Cook 1 hour
Serves 2

Equipment
Casserole

450g (1lb) beef brisket
3 litres (12 cups) water
50g (1¾oz) dried wood ear
    mushroom (black fungus)
200g (7oz) glass (mung bean)
    noodles
1 bunch of spring onions (scallions),
    cut into 5cm (2in) lengths
5 garlic cloves, minced
2 red bird's-eye chillies, chopped
    into 2cm (¾in) pieces
1 tbsp light soy sauce
2 tbsp fish sauce, plus extra for
    seasoning (if required)
3 tbsp gochujang paste
1 tbsp sesame oil
1 tsp black pepper
2 tsp chilli powder of your choice
2 large carrots, peeled and cut into
    thin matchsticks
200g (4 cups) beansprouts

Place the beef brisket in a flameproof casserole and cover with the water. Bring to the boil and then turn down to a simmer and cook for 50 minutes or until tender. During cooking skim off any foam that forms on top of the liquid and discard. Once cooked, remove the beef from the water and place on a plate, leaving the broth in the pan. Allow the beef to cool and then shred.

Meanwhile, place the dried wood ear mushroom (black fungus) in a bowl and pour over boiling water. Allow it to rehydrate for 10 minutes and then drain and chop into strips.

In another bowl, soak the dried noodles in just-boiled water for 10 minutes until soft, then drain and set to one side.

Place the shredded beef in a bowl along with the spring onions (scallions), garlic, red chillies, soy sauce, fish sauce, gochujang paste, sesame oil, black pepper and chilli powder. Combine well and leave to marinate for 20 minutes.

Add the marinated beef back to the now cooled broth and gently bring back up to a simmer. Once simmering, add the carrots, sliced black fungus and beansprouts, cook for 3 minutes, then taste for seasoning and adjust with a splash of fish sauce if required. Add the softened glass noodles, stir to combine and then turn off the heat and serve.

CHILLI PORK BELLY NOODLES

Glass noodles don't carry much flavour of their own, which makes them the perfect starchy accompaniment to this aromatically rich, spicy sauce and soft juicy pork belly pieces.

Prep 20 minutes
Cook 10 minutes
Serves 2

Equipment
Wok

200g (7oz) glass (mung bean) noodles
1 tbsp vegetable oil
8 garlic cloves, minced
8 red bird's-eye chillies, chopped into thin pieces (add less or more depending on how spicy you like your food)
450g (1lb) pork belly, skin removed, thinly sliced
2 tbsp light soy sauce
1 tbsp dark soy sauce
3 tbsp oyster sauce
2 tbsp honey
75g (2½oz) Thai basil leaves

Place the dried noodles in a large bowl and soak them in warm water for 20 minutes until soft. Drain and set to one side.

Heat a wok over a medium heat, add the oil along with the garlic and red chillies and fry until fragrant. Next, add the sliced pork belly and continue to fry for a further 3–4 minutes. Add the light and dark soy sauces, oyster sauce and honey, mix well and then stir in the Thai basil leaves and continue to cook for a further 1–2 minutes. Finally, add the noodles, stir to combine and serve.

SPICY SICHUAN BEEF RICE NOODLES

Tongue-tingling Sichuan pepper combined with the slightly sweet chilli bean paste is the perfect dressing for succulently marinated beef and thick rice noodles.

Prep 10 minutes
Marinate 1 hour
Cook 10 minutes
Serves 2

Equipment
Wok

250g (9oz) beef sirloin, sliced into thin strips
350g (12oz) straight-to-wok thick rice noodles
3 tbsp vegetable oil
3 slices of ginger
3 spring onions (scallions), cut into 5cm (2in) lengths
3 tbsp doubanjiang (fermented chilli bean paste)
1 tsp Sichuan pepper, ground
½ tbsp sugar
200g (4 cups) beansprouts
2 tbsp Chinese rice wine (Shaoxing wine)
pinch of salt, to taste
pinch of white pepper, to taste

For the marinade
½ tsp baking powder
1 tsp dark soy sauce
1 tsp cornflour (cornstarch)
1 tsp sesame oil

Place the beef in a bowl along with the marinade ingredients and mix well. Set to one side to marinate for at least 1 hour.

Soften your noodles under warm water to loosen, drain and set to one side.

Place a wok over a medium-high heat and add half the oil. Once smoking hot, add the beef and sear until browned. Transfer to a plate and set to one side to rest.

Place the wok back over the heat and add the remaining oil. Add the ginger and spring onions and, after around 45 seconds, add the drained rice noodles and fry for about 2 minutes. Add the browned beef along with the doubanjiang, Sichuan pepper and sugar. Fry everything for a further 1–2 minutes, then add the beansprouts and rice wine and cook for another minute, stirring gently to combine all of the ingredients. Finally, taste for seasoning and add a pinch of salt and white pepper if needed.

VEGETABLES

PAN-FRIED COATED TOFU

Crispy pan-fried slabs of tofu in a rich Chinese sauce, perfect served on top of rice, noodles or some lightly stir-fried vegetables, or even better as a side dish.

Prep 10 minutes
Cook 12 minutes
Serves 2–4

Equipment
Wok or frying pan (skillet)

450g (1lb) medium-firm tofu, drained
25g (¼ cup) cornflour (cornstarch)
pinch of salt
2 eggs, beaten
3 tbsp vegetable oil
3 spring onions (scallions), finely chopped
1 tbsp minced ginger
2 garlic cloves, minced
1 tbsp chicken powder (for vegetarian option, use vegetable stock)
250ml (1 cup) water
1 tbsp light soy sauce
1 tbsp oyster sauce (for vegetarian option, replace with mushroom stir-fry sauce)
1 tbsp cornflour (cornstarch) mixed with 2 tbsp water
1 tsp sesame oil

Begin by slicing the tofu into 1cm (½in) thick slabs, then pat dry with kitchen paper or a clean dish towel.

Place the cornflour (cornstarch) and salt on to a plate and dredge each piece of tofu, ensuring they are completely covered. Bang off any excess, then place the dredged tofu into the beaten eggs.

Heat a wok or frying pan (skillet) over a medium-high heat, then add the oil. Once hot, carefully fry the coated tofu for 2–3 minutes until golden brown on both sides, then transfer to a wire rack or kitchen paper to drain.

To the same wok/frying pan, add the chopped spring onions (scallions), ginger and garlic, fry for 30 seconds until fragrant and then add the chicken powder, water, soy sauce and oyster sauce. Bring to a gentle simmer before laying the crispy tofu back into the sauce to cook for a further 5 minutes. Give the cornflour mixture a stir to loosen and carefully stir into your sauce until thick enough to coat the back of a spoon. Once thickened, turn off the heat, drizzle with the sesame oil and serve.

WOK-FRIED AUBERGINE

Here, soft aubergine (eggplant) fingers soak up the garlic and salty soya bean sauce like delicious little sponges.

Prep 5 minutes
Cook 10 minutes
Serves 2

Equipment
Wok

3 large aubergines (eggplants)
2–3 tbsp vegetable oil, plus extra for frying, if needed
5 spring onions (scallions), finely chopped, whites and greens separated
3 garlic cloves, minced
1 tsp grated fresh ginger
2 tbsp soya bean sauce

Begin by cutting the aubergines (eggplants) into fingers of roughly 3 x 12cm (1¼ x 4½in).

Place a wok over a medium-high heat and add the oil. Once hot, add the aubergine slices and fry until golden brown on all sides. Once browned, remove from the wok and set to one side.

Add a little more oil to the wok and add the spring onion (scallion) whites, garlic and ginger. After 30 seconds, add the soya bean sauce and mix well, then add the browned aubergines. Continue to cook, stirring gently and ensuring the aubergines are well dressed with the sauce, then add the spring onion greens. After 1 minute add a splash of water, stir and cook for a further minute, then turn off the heat and serve.

Great with a simple bowl of rice or noodles.

SLOW-BRAISED TOFU WITH CHINESE MUSHROOMS

Tofu and meaty shiitake (poku) mushrooms swimming in a rich soy and wine gravy; you don't have to be vegetarian to enjoy tofu as an ingredient. Made from soya beans it has an exceptional ability to absorb the flavours of a limitless variety of sauces, spices and marinades.

Prep 35 minutes
Cook 25 minutes
Serves 2–4

Equipment
Wok or casserole

8–10 dried Chinese or shiitake (poku) mushrooms
1 tbsp vegetable oil
2 garlic cloves, thinly sliced
60ml (¼ cup) Chinese rice wine (Shaoxing wine)
1 tbsp dark soy sauce
1 tsp light soy sauce
1 tsp sugar
¼ tsp white pepper
340g (11¾oz) pre-fried tofu, cut into bite-sized pieces (available to buy from East Asian supermarkets)
2 tsp cornflour (cornstarch) mixed with 1 tbsp water
2 spring onions (scallions), cut in half and thinly sliced lengthways

Soak the dried mushrooms in a large bowl of just-boiled water. After 30 minutes, drain, reserving 250ml (1 cup) of the water for later, remove the stalks and slice into bite-sized pieces.

Heat a wok or 3–4-litre (13¼–17½-cup) flameproof casserole with the oil, add the mushrooms and garlic and fry for 1–2 minutes. Next, add the reserved cup of mushroom water, the rice wine, dark and light soy sauces, sugar and white pepper. Bring to the boil and add the tofu. Give everything a gentle stir, then turn the heat down to low and cover with a tight lid. After 20 minutes, remove the lid. Give the cornflour (cornstarch) mixture a stir to loosen, then pour into the sauce, mixing continuously until the sauce reaches your desired consistency. Transfer to a serving plate and garnish with the spring onions (scallions).

VEGGIE TOFU STEW

A hearty cross between a potato gratin and spicy veg soup, this stew is a satisfying meal in itself or the perfect accompaniment to freshly steamed rice or thick rice noodles.

Prep 15 minutes
Cook 30 minutes
Serves 2–4

Equipment
Large saucepan

1 onion, finely sliced
1 baking potato, peeled and cut into
    bite-sized pieces
280g (10oz) block medium-firm tofu,
    cut into 1cm (½in) slices
1 litre (4 cups) chicken stock (use
    vegetable stock to make it veggie)
2 tbsp gochujang paste
1 tbsp chilli powder of your choice
2 garlic cloves, minced
1 tsp black pepper
1 tbsp Chinese rice wine
    (Shaoxing wine)
2 tsp sugar
2 tbsp fish sauce (use soy sauce
    or a pinch of salt for seasoning
    to make it veggie)
2 red bird's-eye chillies, roughly
    chopped
5 spring onions (scallions), roughly
    chopped

Layer the onion into the bottom of a 3–4-litre (13¼–17½-cup) saucepan, then add a layer of potato followed by a layer of the tofu and pour over enough of the stock so that it just covers the tofu.

Combine the gochujang paste with the chilli powder, garlic, black pepper, rice wine, sugar and fish sauce. Mix well and then spoon on top of the tofu.

Place the saucepan over a medium heat and gently bring to a simmer. Cover with a lid and cook for 20 minutes or until the potatoes are tender. Sprinkle with the chopped chillies and spring onions (scallions) and cook for a further 6–8 minutes to infuse.

Spoon into deep bowls and serve hot.

SAUCY VEGETABLE NOODLES

Crisp fresh vegetables and springy egg noodles in a smooth fragrant sauce, abundant in texture and flavour and enough to satisfy vegetarians and carnivores alike.

Prep 10 minutes
Cook 8 minutes
Serves 2

Equipment
Wok

1 tbsp light soy sauce
1 tsp sugar
1 tbsp Chinese rice wine
  (Shaoxing wine)
2 tbsp water
3 tbsp hoisin sauce
1 tbsp vegetable oil
1 garlic clove, minced
3 spring onions (scallions), chopped
  into 5cm (2in) lengths
1 red (bell) pepper, deseeded and
  cut into strips
1 small carrot, peeled and sliced
200g (7oz) mushrooms of your
  choice, sliced
450g (1lb) straight-to-wok medium
  thick egg noodles
150g (5oz) mangetout (snowpeas),
  cut in half lengthways
150g (5oz) choy sum, chopped into
  bite-sized pieces
1 tsp sesame oil

In a small bowl, combine the soy sauce, sugar, rice wine, water and hoisin sauce. Set to one side.

Heat a wok over a medium-high heat and add the vegetable oil. Once hot, add the garlic and half of the spring onions and mix, then add the red pepper, carrot and mushrooms. Once these have seared and softened, add the noodles. Give everything a good mix and cook for 1–2 minutes, then add the mangetout (snowpeas). Once everything is combined, give your sauce mixture a quick stir and add it to the wok. Stir to combine all the ingredients and then add the choy sum. Continue to stir-fry for a further 45 seconds, then turn off the heat and stir through the sesame oil. Transfer to a serving plate and garnish with the remaining spring onions.

EASY VEGGIE SATAY NOODLES

The fastest satay noodles ever! Share with a friend or just grab your chopsticks and dive in.

Prep 5 minutes
Cook 4 minutes
Serves 2

Equipment
Large saucepan

2 nests dried egg noodles
1 spring onion (scallion), finely sliced
½ red (bell) pepper, deseeded and
   cut into matchsticks
¼ cucumber, cut into matchsticks

For the sauce
2 garlic cloves, grated
2 tbsp light soy sauce
2 heaped tbsp crunchy peanut
   butter
3 tbsp hot water
½ tbsp sugar
pinch of salt

Combine all the sauce ingredients together in a serving bowl and set to one side.

Heat a 2–3-litre (8¾–13¼-cup) saucepan of water over a medium-high heat and, once boiling, add the noodles and cook until tender. Drain and add to the serving bowl containing the sauce and toss together. Garnish with the spring onion (scallion), red (bell) pepper and cucumber.

CHARRED SPRING ONION UDON

Char spring onions (scallions) to release their natural sugars and coat them in delicious aromatic flavours to accompany simply succulent udon noodles.

Prep 5 minutes
Cook 4 minutes
Serves 2

Equipment
Wok

300g (10oz) straight-to-wok
   udon noodles
60ml (¼ cup) water
2 tbsp light soy sauce
1 tbsp dark soy sauce
½ tbsp black rice vinegar
1 tbsp Chinese rice wine
   (Shaoxing wine)
2 tbsp vegetable oil
2 bunches of spring onions
   (scallions), greens roughly
   chopped into 5cm (2in) lengths,
   whites crushed
1 tbsp minced ginger
1 tbsp minced garlic

Place the noodles in a colander or sieve (strainer) and loosen under hot water. Drain and set to one side.

In a bowl, mix together the water, light and dark soy sauces, vinegar and rice wine and set to one side.

Place a wok over a medium-high heat, add the oil and, once hot, add the chopped and crushed spring onions (scallions), allowing them to fry and char lightly before stirring. Once the spring onions are well charred all over, add the ginger and garlic and fry until fragrant. Next, add the drained noodles and toss to combine with the cooked aromatics. Add the sauce mixture, stir through and, once everything is piping hot, serve immediately.

SWEET CHILLI GARLIC RICE

This fried rice is potent with garlic and slightly sweet against a backdrop of hot chilli.

Prep 5 minutes
Cook 10 minutes
Serves 2–3

Equipment
Wok

2 tbsp vegetable oil
1 onion, finely diced
8 garlic cloves, roughly chopped
2 red bird's-eye chillies, roughly chopped
500g (1lb 2oz) cooked long-grain or basmati rice
3 spring onions (scallions), finely sliced, whites and greens separated
4 tbsp sweet chilli sauce
salt, to taste

Place a wok over a medium-high heat, add the oil and, once smoking, add the onion and garlic. Fry until golden brown and soft but be careful not to let the garlic burn, as it will turn bitter. Next, add the chillies and fry for a further 30–40 seconds until fragrant. Then add the cooked rice and spring onion (scallion) whites and continue to fry for 2–3 minutes; you want the rice grains to toast slightly, which will give your dish a slightly nutty flavour, so don't stir the ingredients constantly. Once the rice is fully heated through, taste and season with salt to your liking. Stir in the sweet chilli sauce and cook for a further minute to ensure the sauce is hot. Remove from the heat, sprinkle over the spring onion greens and serve.

SPICY SINGAPORE VEGETABLE RICE

Pretty much 'anything goes' when it comes to fried rice, but a simple Chinese takeaway classic is the Spicy Singapore-style with its signature curry powder taste.

Prep 5 minutes
Cook 10 minutes
Serves 2–3

Equipment
Wok

2 tbsp vegetable oil
1 onion, finely diced
2 garlic cloves, roughly chopped
2 red bird's-eye chillies, roughly chopped
500g (1lb 2oz) cooked long-grain or basmati rice
150g (5oz) frozen mixed baby vegetables, defrosted
2 tbsp Chinese curry powder, or use your favourite
1 tbsp light soy sauce
1 tsp dark soy sauce
pinch of white pepper
salt, to taste

Place a wok over a medium-high heat, add the oil and, once smoking, add the onion and garlic and fry until golden brown, being careful not to let the garlic burn. Add the chopped chillies and fry for a further 30 seconds until fragrant, then add the cooked rice and continue to fry for 2–3 minutes; you want the rice grains to toast slightly, which will give your dish a slightly nutty flavour, so don't stir the ingredients constantly. Now add the thawed frozen vegetables along with the curry powder, light and dark soy sauces and white pepper and toss gently to combine with the rice. Once the ingredients are fully heated through, taste the rice and adjust the seasoning with salt if required. Serve piping hot.

CHICKEN & DUCK

COCONUT CHICKEN CURRY SOUP

With a classic Thai flavour profile, the lemongrass notes in the red curry paste sing in sweet harmony with the creamy coconut milk and salty fish sauce to create a perfectly balanced noodle soup.

Prep 5 minutes
Cook 10 minutes
Serves 2

Equipment
Wok

2 tbsp vegetable oil
1½ tbsp minced garlic
1 tbsp grated ginger
3 tbsp Thai red curry paste
250g (9oz) chicken breast, sliced into bite-sized pieces
1.2 litres (5 cups) chicken stock
400ml (14fl oz) can coconut milk
3 tbsp fish sauce
150g (5oz) thin rice noodles
150g (3 cups) beansprouts
salt and white pepper, to taste

Place a wok over a medium-high heat, add the oil along with the garlic, ginger and red curry paste and fry for 1–2 minutes until fragrant and sizzling. Add the sliced chicken, stir to coat in the paste and spread out across the wok to cook. Once the chicken is cooked, add the chicken stock, coconut milk and fish sauce and bring to the boil. Add the rice noodles and beansprouts and bring back to the boil. Taste and adjust the seasoning to your liking with salt and white pepper. Serve.

SPATCHCOCK TERIYAKI CHICKEN

Turn your basic roast chicken on its head with this sticky sweet teriyaki marinade.

Prep 10 minutes
Cook 1 hour 20 minutes
Serves 2–4

Equipment
Baking dish

1 whole chicken, backbone removed and flattened (see Tip)
2 tbsp vegetable oil
pinch of salt
pinch of black pepper

For the marinade
3 tbsp mirin
3 tbsp light soy sauce
1 tbsp dark soy sauce
2 tbsp brown sugar
2 tsp grated ginger
2 tsp grated garlic
2 tbsp hoisin sauce
½ tsp Chinese five spice

Preheat the oven to 170°C (340°F).

Brush the chicken on both sides with the oil and then season with salt and black pepper. Lay flat in a 33 x 23cm (13 x 9in) baking dish (skin-side up) and place into the hot oven.

Combine all the marinade ingredients in a bowl and set to one side.

After 20 minutes of cooking, brush the chicken on both sides with some of the marinade. Return to the oven for a further 40–50 minutes, basting with more marinade every 10 minutes to build up the layers. Once the chicken has cooked all the way through – you can check by inserting a skewer in the thickest part and if the juices run clear, you're good to go – pour over the remaining marinade and cook for a final 10 minutes.

Serve with a green salad, noodles or rice.

Kwoklyn's tip
To spatchcock a chicken, place the chicken on a chopping board, breast-side down, with the legs towards you. Splay the chicken and then, using a sharp knife, remove the backbone by pressing down firmly along each side of the spine to cut through the rib bones. Remove the bone. Turn the chicken over and flatten it with the heel of your hand. Wash your hands and equipment thoroughly.

SRIRACHA ROASTED CHICKEN THIGHS

Juicy and spicy through and through with a tantalizingly crispy skin.

Prep 10 minutes
Marinate 2 hours
Cook 1 hour
Serves 2–4

Equipment
Large roasting tray (sheet pan)

450g (1lb) bone-in chicken thighs (you can use boneless if you prefer)
2 sweet red (bell) peppers, deseeded and cut into bite-sized pieces
1 onion, diced
5 spring onions (scallions), cut into 5cm (2in) lengths
1 tsp salt
1 tsp garlic powder
1 tsp ground ginger
1 tsp chilli powder of your choice
1 tbsp light soy sauce
3 tbsp Sriracha chilli sauce
1 tbsp honey

Combine all the ingredients in a 33 x 23cm (13 x 9in) roasting tray (sheet pan), massaging the marinade fully into the chicken thighs and the vegetables, ensuring they are all well covered. Allow to marinate for 2 hours.

Preheat the oven to 170°C (340°F).

Place the roasting tray into the hot oven and after 20 minutes give everything a turn in the tray, place back into the oven and cook for a further 20–30 minutes. Once the chicken is fully cooked, increase the oven temperature to 200°C (400°F), turn all of the chicken thighs skin-side up in the tray and cook for a further 10 minutes to achieve a crispy skin.

Remove from the oven and serve.

SICHUAN DUCK PIZZA

'Pizza is a healthy option,' said no-one ever, yet I could practically live off these and pretty much did in the mid to late 1990s! You 'can' make your own Sichuan or aromatic duck but for this recipe I bought one ready-made, which came with a little sachet of sauce and pancakes and I just popped those into my freezer for another time.

Prep 30 minutes, plus 20 minutes resting
Cook 15 minutes per pizza
Serves 2–6

Equipment
Baking sheet
Stand mixer (optional)

540g (1lb 3oz) or ½ aromatic duck
8 spring onions (scallions), shredded
½ cucumber, cut into matchsticks
250ml (1 cup) hoisin sauce
1kg (2lb 4oz) grated mozzarella

For the dough
1kg (8 cups) strong white bread flour, plus extra for dusting
1 tbsp caster sugar
14g (1 tbsp) instant yeast
1 tsp salt
650ml (2⅓ cups) warm water
4 tbsp olive oil

Remove the duck meat from the bones and shred it into small pieces and chunks. Set this to one side with the spring onions (scallions) and cucumber.

Sift the flour into the bowl of a stand mixer fitted with the dough hook attachment, add the sugar and yeast and mix well, then add the salt and mix again. Turn the mixer on to the low setting and begin to add the water and olive oil gradually as it mixes. Once all of the liquid has been added, turn the mixer up a level and knead until you have a springy dough. Turn off the mixer, cover the dough with clingfilm (plastic wrap) and allow it to rest for 20 minutes.

If you don't have a stand mixer, combine the dough ingredients in the same order but simply knead by hand.

Flour a worktop and separate the dough into 4–6 pieces. Roll out each piece of dough into a disc about 30cm (12in) in diameter.

Preheat the oven to 230°C (450°F).

Take one of the bases and generously spread with hoisin sauce, then arrange the cucumber, spring onion and duck on top and sprinkle with mozzarella cheese.

Place on to a baking sheet and into your very hot oven for 12–15 minutes or until golden brown and bubbling. Repeat with the remaining dough and toppings. Serve and enjoy.

MACANESE-STYLE CHICKEN CURRY

Macanese-style chicken curry, or *Po Kok Gai*, is a Chinese fusion Macanese- and Portuguese-style chicken dish. Mildly spicy, it is a slightly sweet chicken curry with a creamy coconut sauce.

Prep 10 minutes
Marinate 30 minutes
Cook 45 minutes
Serves 2–4

Equipment
Casserole or clay pot

450g (1lb) chicken thighs, drumsticks or breasts (cut into 3 pieces), ideally bone-in, skin on
2 tbsp olive oil
1 onion, sliced
2 large waxy potatoes, peeled and cut into 4cm (1½in) cubes
2 carrots, peeled and sliced
2 tbsp medium curry powder
3 tbsp ground turmeric
400ml (14fl oz) can coconut milk
250ml (1 cup) chicken stock
salt and pepper, to taste

For the marinade
1½ tbsp Chinese rice wine (Shaoxing wine)
1 tbsp ginger juice (grate a thumb-sized piece of ginger and squeeze)
1½ tbsp sugar
3 tbsp light soy sauce

Place all the marinade ingredients in a large bowl, add the chicken, mix well, cover and allow to marinate for 30 minutes.

Heat the oil in a 4–5-litre (17½–22-cup) flameproof casserole or clay pot over a medium-high heat, then add the chicken and cook for 8 minutes, browning all sides (reserve any leftover marinade). Transfer the chicken to a plate and set to one side, then add the onion to the pot and fry for 2–3 minutes until softened and browned. Add the potatoes, carrots, curry powder and turmeric. Mix thoroughly and cook for a further 2 minutes until the air becomes fragrant. Add the coconut milk, reserved marinade and top up with enough chicken stock to cover the ingredients. Lastly pop in the browned chicken, not forgetting to also pour in any juices that may have gathered on the plate.

Bring to the boil and then turn down to a simmer, cover with a lid and cook for 20 minutes. Remove the lid; if the chicken has dried out, add a little more water to create a sauce, but if there is a lot of liquid, leave the lid off and allow the sauce to reduce until you have reached your desired consistency. Add salt and pepper to taste and serve.

SOY-GLAZED ROAST CHICKEN

The dark glazed chicken, oozing with classic Cantonese flavours, is undeniably the star of this particular show, but the vegetable understudies are well worth a credit for their flavoursome support of the roasting bird.

Prep 20 minutes
Marinate 2 hours
Cook 1 hour 20 minutes, plus 20 minutes resting
Serves 2–4

Equipment
Casserole or clay pot

1 whole chicken, about 1.5–2kg (3lb 5oz–4lb 8oz)
8 carrots, peeled
6 potatoes, peeled and cut into large pieces
10–12 shallots, peeled

For the marinade
thumb-sized piece of ginger, smashed
2 garlic cloves, crushed
3 spring onions (scallions), roughly chopped
2 star anise
1 tsp Chinese five spice
3 tbsp Chinese rice wine (Shaoxing wine)
3 tbsp light soy sauce
2 tbsp dark soy sauce
3 tbsp maltose or honey
2 tsp chicken powder
170ml (⅔ cup) water
1 tbsp vegetable oil

Mix together all the marinade ingredients in a large bowl and, using your hands, rub the marinade all over the chicken, ensuring it is well coated, including inside the cavity. Leave the chicken breast-side down in the bowl and place in the fridge for 1 hour, then baste the chicken with the marinade again and this time leave it breast-side up for another hour out of the fridge.

Preheat the oven to 180°C (350°F).

Place the carrots, potatoes and shallots in the bottom of a 4–5-litre (17½–22-cup) flameproof casserole or clay pot, then lay the chicken breast-side up on top of the veggies and pour any liquid marinade over the chicken, ensuring you coat inside the cavity by tipping the chicken on its end and drizzling marinade inside. Pop on the lid and place into the oven to cook for 1 hour 20 minutes, basting the bird every 15 minutes. Keep an eye on the glaze, as you may need to add a little more water to prevent it from completely drying out in the pot.

Once the chicken has achieved a rich brown colour and is cooked all the way through, remove from the oven and allow to stand for 20 minutes before serving with the veggies and a heaping pot of steamed rice.

ONE-POT LEMON CHICKEN

Fresh sticky lemon glaze on juicy chicken thighs: so full of flavour but with such minimal prep you could almost believe this dish cooks itself.

Prep 5 minutes
Cook 45 minutes–1 hour
(pressure cooker vs casserole)
Serves 2–4

Equipment
Casserole or pressure cooker

500g (1lb 2oz) skin-on chicken thighs
(boneless optional)
pinch of salt
pinch of black pepper
1 tbsp vegetable oil
2 garlic cloves, minced
2 tbsp Chinese rice wine
(Shaoxing wine)
2 tsp chicken powder
250ml (1 cup) water
2 tbsp cornflour (cornstarch)
1 tbsp light soy sauce
2 tsp dark soy sauce
1 lemon: juice of ½; ½ sliced
3 tbsp honey
1 tsp dried sage
1 tsp dried thyme

Begin by seasoning the chicken thighs with the salt and black pepper, then heat a 3–4-litre (13¼–17½-cup) flameproof casserole or pressure cooker over a medium heat and add the vegetable oil. Place the thighs into the hot oil, skin-side down, and cook for 3–4 minutes. Once browned, turn the pieces of chicken over and cook for a further 3–4 minutes.

Next, add the garlic and fry for 30 seconds or until fragrant and then add the Chinese rice wine to deglaze the bottom of the pan. Sprinkle in the chicken powder, mix, then add the water and stir again.

In a separate bowl, combine the cornflour (cornstarch), light and dark soy sauces, lemon juice and honey and, once combined, add to the chicken along with the sliced lemon. Place the lid on the pot and continue to cook on low for 30 minutes in a pressure cooker or for 45 minutes in a casserole. Your sauce should be thick and glossy and coat the chicken once cooked. You may find that you need to add a little more water to loosen the finished sauce if cooking in a casserole. Finally, sprinkle over the dried sage and thyme and mix through. Serve with freshly cooked steamed rice.

'THREE-CUP' HOT-POT CHICKEN

Hot-pot cooking enables you to cook the ingredients inside without losing any moisture, creating a tender and flavourful dish. The name 'Three Cup' refers to an old Chinese and Taiwanese dish where a cup each of soy sauce, rice wine and sesame oil were used; I've adapted my recipe to use less than the original as one cup of each would be enough to cook a bucketload of chicken!

Prep 5 minutes, plus 30 minutes soaking
Cook 30 minutes
Serves 2–4

Equipment
Clay pot or casserole

450g (1lb) boneless chicken thighs, skin on
1 tsp salt
1 tbsp white rice vinegar
1 tbsp vegetable oil
thumb-sized piece of ginger, peeled and cut into thin matchsticks
3 garlic cloves, thinly sliced
2 spring onions (scallions), finely sliced, whites and greens separated
2 tbsp light soy sauce
2 tbsp dark soy sauce
60ml (¼ cup) chicken stock
2 tbsp honey
2 tbsp Chinese rice wine (Shaoxing wine)
handful of Thai basil leaves
1 tbsp sesame oil

Place the chicken in a bowl, add the salt and white rice vinegar and enough water to cover the chicken completely. Allow to soak for 30 minutes. This process will help remove any impurities from the chicken and loosen the muscle fibres.

Drain the chicken and pat dry with kitchen paper.

Heat the vegetable oil in a 3–4-litre (13¼–17½-cup) clay pot or flameproof casserole over a medium heat, add the chicken thighs, skin-side down, and fry for 3–4 minutes until golden. Turn the chicken over and fry the other side for a further 3 minutes. Next, add the ginger, garlic and spring onion (scallion) whites and stir-fry until aromatic. Add the light and dark soy sauces, chicken stock, honey and Chinese rice wine. Mix well, then cover and simmer over a low heat for 20 minutes. Gently stir in the Thai basil leaves and sesame oil and serve garnished with the spring onion greens.

GLAZED STICKY PEPPER CHICKEN

Melt-in-the-mouth chicken in a rich peppery sauce.

Prep 5 minutes
Cook 50 minutes
Serves 2–4

Equipment
Clay pot

1 tbsp vegetable oil
600g (1lb 5oz) chicken thighs,
  bone-in and skin on
2 tbsp freshly cracked black pepper
125ml (½ cup) dark soy sauce
125ml (½ cup) water
3 spring onions (scallions), roughly
  cut into rings

Heat a 2–3-litre (8¾–13¼-cup) clay pot over a medium-high heat, add the oil and fry the chicken for 5 minutes, browning and sealing each side. Remove the chicken and discard the oil, except for ½ tablespoon. Return the chicken to the pot, add the black pepper, soy sauce and water and stir to coat each piece well. Bring to the boil, then turn the heat down to medium-low, place a lid on the pot and allow to simmer for 40 minutes, turning the chicken once during cooking. Sprinkle with the chopped spring onions (scallions) and serve hot with salad, noodles or rice.

SALT-POACHED CHICKEN

If asked to sum up my childhood in one dish, then this has to be it. Poppa Wan would chop the cooked Salt Chicken into pieces and place them into a bowl. The bowl of chicken would then sit on a wire rack in the rice cooker to reheat while the rice cooked, and the bowl would collect the juices as they steamed. Poured over soft sticky Chinese rice with a splash of soy sauce for colour, this is my idea of food heaven!

Prep 10 minutes
Cook 1 hour
Serves 5–6

Equipment
Large saucepan
Digital thermometer

1 whole chicken, about 1.8–2.2kg (4–4lb 15oz)
thumb-sized piece of ginger, peeled and sliced
3 spring onions (scallions), bruised
6–7 litres (24–28 cups) water, or as much as needed
340g (11¾oz) large-grain salt

To remove any unwanted juices from the chicken, dab it with kitchen paper and dispose of the kitchen paper right away. Then stuff with the sliced ginger and bruised spring onions (scallions). In a 10-litre (10-quart) saucepan over a high heat, bring the water and the salt to the boil. Place the chicken into the boiling water, breast-side up. If the bird isn't completely covered, top up with more boiling water. Bring the water back to a simmer, cover and adjust the heat so it is barely simmering.

Cook the chicken for 40 minutes. Once cooked, carefully remove the chicken, ensuring you drain the water from the cavity. If you have a meat thermometer, insert through the centre of the thickest part of the breast – if it reads 75°C (167°F) or above the chicken is cooked. If the chicken requires further cooking, place back into the pan, cover and cook for a further 5 minutes before testing again.

Once the chicken has finished cooking, immerse it into a large bowl of iced water for 3 minutes. This will help tighten the skin of the chicken and stop any further cooking. Drain and allow to rest for 10 minutes.

Cut the chicken into pieces and serve.

Kwoklyn's tip
Mum always had her chicken with a bowl of ginger paste. While the bird is resting grate 85g (3oz) ginger into a heatproof bowl and add ½ teaspoon table salt. Heat 3 tablespoons of vegetable oil in a small saucepan until it is just beginning to smoke, then carefully pour the oil into the bowl of ginger and salt and mix well. Be careful as it will sizzle and spit, but the smell will be fantastic.

SLOW-COOKED PLUM DUCK

Tender duck legs in a sumptuous sweet and tangy plum sauce. Not exactly a quick fix, but well worth the wait.

Prep 10 minutes
Cook 3 hours 40 minutes
Serves 4

Equipment
Casserole

4 whole duck legs
1 large onion, sliced
6 spring onions (scallions), whites cut into 5cm (2in) lengths, greens cut into rings
2 garlic cloves, minced
2cm (¾in) piece of ginger, peeled and minced
½ tsp Chinese five spice
2 star anise
1½ tbsp chicken powder
1 tbsp tomato purée (paste)
2 tbsp plain (all-purpose) flour
500ml (2 cups) water
1 tbsp white rice vinegar
3 tbsp honey
125ml (½ cup) hoisin sauce
60ml (¼ cup) plum jam
4 plums, halved and pitted

Heat a 3–4-litre (13¼–17½-cup) flameproof casserole over a medium heat and dry-fry the duck legs until the fat starts to run out of them. Increase the heat to high and brown the legs on both sides. Remove from the pan and set to one side.

Preheat the oven to 110°C (225°F).

Discard the excess duck fat, except for 1 tablespoon, then add the onion and fry until it has softened. Then add the spring onion (scallion) whites, garlic and ginger and fry for another minute. Add the Chinese five spice, star anise and chicken powder, mix and then add the tomato purée (paste). Mix again and fry for another minute, then add the flour and continue to stir until all of the ingredients are coated. Add the water slowly, mixing the entire time to avoid creating lumps, then stir in the vinegar, honey and hoisin sauce. Once everything is thoroughly combined, add the plum jam and stir until it melts into the sauce, then add the plums. Stir gently to submerge and finally place the duck legs back into the pot. Put the lid on and place into the preheated oven to cook for 3½ hours.

Once cooked, transfer to a serving dish and garnish with the spring onion greens before serving with rice or noodles.

CHINESE CHICKEN CURRY ONE-POT

One of the most ordered dishes of any Chinese takeaway anywhere, made simple. Delicious served over boiled rice, fried rice, chow mein, chips or even a baked potato.

Prep 10 minutes
Cook 40 minutes
Serves 2–4

Equipment
Casserole or large saucepan

1 tbsp vegetable oil
450g (1lb) chicken thighs, drumsticks or breasts (cut into 3 pieces), ideally bone-in, skin on
1 large onion, cut into 2.5cm (1in) dice
2 large carrots, peeled and sliced
3 garlic cloves, roughly chopped
3 celery sticks, diced
2 tbsp Chinese curry powder (or use your favourite depending how hot you like it)
2 tbsp chicken powder
1 litre (4 cups) water
2 tbsp light soy sauce
1 tbsp honey or sugar
2 bay leaves
100g (3½oz) button mushrooms, cut into bite-sized pieces
60g (½ cup) frozen peas
1 tsp garam masala
2 tbsp cornflour (cornstarch) mixed with 4 tbsp water
salt and pepper

Add the oil to a 4–5-litre (17½–22-cup) flameproof casserole or large saucepan, add the chicken and cook for 5 minutes, browning all sides. Next, add the onion, carrot, garlic and celery sticks and continue to fry for a further 2 minutes until starting to soften and become fragrant.

Sprinkle in the curry powder and chicken powder, mix well, then add the water, soy sauce, honey and bay leaves and stir to combine. Bring to the boil, then turn down to a simmer, place the lid on the pan and cook for 25 minutes.

Remove the lid, add the mushrooms and bring back up to the boil. Once boiling, reduce the heat to medium and cook the mushrooms until tender, then add the peas and garam masala and stir. Give your cornflour (cornstarch) mixture a stir to loosen and slowly pour into the curry sauce, stirring constantly to thicken. Finally, remove the bay leaves (no one wants to chow down on those), taste to check the seasoning and adjust with salt and pepper if required.

Kwoklyn's tip
If you prefer a smoother curry sauce, remove the chicken pieces and bay leaves after the 25 minutes cooking is done and, before adding the mushrooms, blend the sauce and veggies to a smooth consistency, then replace the chicken and carry on with the recipe as above.

RICE COOKER CANTONESE CHICKEN

Layers of homely goodness cooked to perfection at just the flick of a switch! The Cantonese aromatics of garlic, ginger and spring onion release their juices to flavour the chicken and rice as they harmoniously steam together.

Prep 30 minutes
Cook 35 minutes
Serves 2

Equipment
Rice cooker

2 boneless, skinless chicken breasts
  or chicken thighs, cut into
  2–3 pieces (small enough
  to fit in the rice cooker)
pinch of salt
pinch of white pepper
180g (1 cup) Thai fragrant rice
  (or long-grain rice)
250ml (1 cup) chicken stock
1 tbsp vegetable oil
thumb-sized piece of ginger,
  peeled and roughly sliced
3 spring onions (scallions),
  roughly chopped
2 garlic cloves, roughly chopped

Season the chicken with the salt and white pepper and set to one side.

Place the rice in a bowl and wash 2–3 times until the water becomes less cloudy, cover with water and allow to soak for 30 minutes. Once soaked, pour off the excess water and place into a rice cooker. Pour over the chicken stock and oil. Lay the chicken, ginger, spring onions (scallions) and garlic over the top of the rice (do not stir). Put on the lid and click your rice cooker on to cook – usually for about 20 minutes. Once the cooker clicks off, allow it to stand for a further 5–10 minutes before serving.

BOOZY CHICKEN SOUP

So named for the ample helpings of Chinese rice wine and brandy! Technically a soup but I highly recommend that you have some freshly steamed Thai fragrant rice heaped in your serving bowls ready to be swamped with your chicken broth.

Prep 5 minutes
Cook 50 minutes
Serves 2

Equipment
Wok

2 tbsp vegetable oil
2 thumb-sized pieces of ginger, peeled and roughly sliced
450g (1lb) skinless chicken thighs (you can use boneless if you prefer)
1 tbsp chicken powder
750ml (3 cups) Chinese rice wine (Shaoxing wine)
2 tbsp brandy
pinch of salt
pinch of white pepper
pinch of sugar
5 spring onions (scallions), cut into 5cm (2in) lengths
1 tbsp sesame oil

Heat a wok over a medium-high heat, add the oil and ginger and fry for 45 seconds or until fragrant. Add the chicken thighs and allow to gently brown for 8–10 minutes. Add the chicken powder, pour in the Chinese rice wine and brandy and bring to the boil. Allow to boil for a couple of minutes, then add 1.25 litres (5 cups) of water along with the salt, white pepper and sugar. Bring back to the boil, then reduce the heat and simmer for 30 minutes. During the cooking process you may find that a foam forms on the top of the soup, skim this off and discard. Once the chicken is fully cooked, add the spring onions (scallions) and cook for a further 2–3 minutes, then taste and adjust the seasoning to your liking.

Ladle the soup into serving bowls and drizzle with the sesame oil. Serve as it is, or with freshly steamed rice, if you like.

PORK & BEEF

SILKEN TOFU EGGS

Delicately tender silken tofu with salty Spam and fluffy steamed egg, drizzled in a rich savoury sauce. There are many variations of this dish using different classic Chinese sauces and for a quick fix you could easily just swap out the sauce for your favourite chilli oil.

Prep 10 minutes
Cook 5 minutes
Serves 2

Equipment
Wok (with a lid)

340g (11¾oz) silken tofu, drained
   and cut into 3 x 2 x 1cm
   (1¼ x ¾ x ½in) slices
3 eggs, beaten
200g (7oz) Spam, cut into 1cm
   (½in) cubes
1 tbsp light soy sauce
2 tbsp oyster sauce
1 tsp chicken powder
3 tbsp water
1 tsp sesame oil
2 spring onions (scallions),
   finely chopped

Place the silken tofu into a lidded non-stick wok and gently spread over the base of the wok. Pour over the beaten eggs and sprinkle with the diced Spam. Place on the lid and steam for 2–3 minutes over a medium-low heat until the eggs have set. In a separate bowl, mix the soy sauce, oyster sauce, chicken powder, water and sesame oil, then pour this over the steamed tofu eggs. Finally, sprinkle with the chopped spring onions (scallions).

Serve with rice or noodles or on its own.

PORK BELLY ADOBO

Originating from the Philippines, adobo comes in many taste variations, but all have three ingredients in common: vinegar, garlic and black pepper. You might think that the huge glug of vinegar will make the dish too acidic but this is perfectly balanced by the sugar. Adobo is a dish of bold flavours and is perfect heaped over starchy white rice or potatoes.

Prep 5 minutes
Marinate 2 hours +
Cook 1 hour 15 minutes
Serves 2–4

Equipment
Wok or saucepan

500g (1lb 2oz) pork belly, cut into 2.5cm (1in) chunks
2 garlic cloves, roughly chopped
125ml (½ cup) light soy sauce
1 tbsp fish sauce
1 tbsp vegetable oil
½ tbsp crushed black peppercorns
5 bay leaves
2 tbsp muscovado sugar
500ml (2 cups) water
5 tbsp white rice vinegar

Place the pork in a bowl with the garlic, soy sauce and fish sauce, massage it all together to ensure all of the pork is thoroughly coated, cover and place in the fridge to marinate for at least 2 hours or preferably overnight.

Remove the pork from the marinade, reserving the liquid.

Heat a wok or saucepan over a medium-high heat, add the oil and marinated pork and cook until golden brown on all sides. Pour in the remaining marinade, peppercorns, bay leaves, sugar and water, turn down to a simmer and cook for a further 1 hour. Pour in the vinegar and cook for a further 10 minutes.

Serve as you like, with freshly steamed rice or even a big pile of mashed potatoes.

PORK CONGEE

A gentle breakfast treat, perfect for those days when your body is maybe telling you that it needs just a little more care and attention than usual. For me, a big bowl served steaming hot and drizzled with light soy sauce and a smattering of peanuts is the way to go.

Prep 15 minutes
Cook 1 hour 40 minutes
Serves 4

Equipment
Large saucepan

75g (½ cup) Chinese pickled turnip (optional)
180g (1 cup) long-grain rice
2 litres (8 cups) water or vegetable stock
125g (4½oz) pork, cut into matchsticks (I use pork loin but my dad likes pork shoulder)
thumb-sized piece of ginger, peeled and thinly sliced
salt and white pepper

Toppings (optional)
crushed salted peanuts
spring onions (scallions), thinly sliced
deep-fried crispy onion
sesame seeds
light soy sauce
crispy tofu pieces

If you are using the pickled turnip, rinse under cold water to remove some of the salt and cut into bite-sized matchsticks.

Rinse the rice until the water is no longer cloudy and drain.

In a 3–4-litre (13¼–17½-cup) saucepan, place the rice, water or stock, pork, ginger and pickled turnip (if using), bring to the boil, then turn down to a simmer and cook for about 1½ hours. If it looks like the rice is becoming too thick, you can add more water, as the congee should be of pouring consistency.

Season to taste with salt and white pepper, then serve hot with your favourite toppings.

STEAMED EGG AND PORK

Dad cooked this dish a lot when we were young. The smell instantly transports me back to our little council house and visions of Dad slurping up the egg and rice as he watched his Chinese programmes on VHS.

Prep 40 minutes
Cook 15 minutes
Serves 2–4

Equipment
Bamboo steamer

3–5 dried Chinese or shiitake (poku)
   mushrooms
200g (7oz) minced (ground) pork
2 spring onions (scallions),
   finely sliced
3 eggs
600ml (2½ cups) water
pinch of salt and white pepper

For the marinade
¼ tsp salt
1 tsp sugar
pinch of white pepper (to taste)
1 tbsp cornflour (cornstarch)
1 tbsp light soy sauce
1 tbsp sesame oil
2cm (¾in) piece of dried orange
   peel, broken into small pieces

Place the dried mushrooms in a bowl and cover with boiling water to rehydrate.

While the mushrooms are soaking, mix all the marinade ingredients together in another bowl.

After 30 minutes the mushrooms should have softened; remove from the liquid, pat dry, then remove and discard the hard stalks. Thinly slice the mushrooms and add to the marinade along with the pork and spring onions (scallions) and mix well.

Whisk the eggs in a bowl, then add the water and stir together.

Pour the pork mixture into an ovenproof ceramic baking dish (one that will fit inside your steamer), distributing it evenly. Gently pour the egg mixture over the top and season with the salt and white pepper.

Place the dish into a 25cm (10in) bamboo steamer and steam on high for 15 minutes. Serve immediately with rice.

ROASTED BARBECUE RIBS

A true crowd-pleaser! Fall-off-the-bone rib meat and moreishly sticky sauce is a deliciously messy affair and if your guests aren't wearing the sauce like a toddler with ice cream, they're just not eating these ribs properly...

Prep 5 minutes, plus 30 minutes
   soaking
Marinate 2 hours
Cook 2 hours 10 minutes
Serves 4

Equipment
Large roasting tray (sheet pan)

1.8kg (4lb) pork ribs on the rack
1 tsp salt
1 tbsp white rice vinegar
1 tbsp cornflour (cornstarch) mixed
   with 2 tbsp water

For the sauce
5 garlic cloves, crushed
3 slices of ginger
3 spring onions (scallions),
   left whole
3 star anise
1 cinnamon stick
250ml (1 cup) hoisin sauce
250ml (1 cup) yellow bean sauce
100g (½ cup) granulated sugar
2 tbsp Chinese five spice
2 tbsp chicken powder
1 litre (4 cups) water

Place the rack of ribs in a large bowl, add the salt and vinegar and cover with water. Allow to soak for at least 30 minutes; this process will help remove any impurities and will tenderize the ribs. Drain and pat dry with kitchen paper or a clean dish towel.

Combine all the sauce ingredients (except the water) in a 33 x 23cm (13 x 9in) roasting tray (sheet pan), then add the ribs and massage the sauce thoroughly into the ribs. Allow to marinate for 2 hours.

Preheat the oven to 160°C (325°F).

Pour the water into the tray of ribs and combine gently with the sauce. Cover the roasting tray tightly with foil, place into the oven and roast for 1½ hours. Then increase the oven temperature to 180°C (350°F), uncover the ribs and continue to roast for a further 30 minutes uncovered, basting the ribs every 10 minutes. Now stir the cornflour (cornstarch) mixture into the sauce, ensuring it is well combined, then place the ribs back into the oven for a final 10 minutes to allow the sauce to thicken.

MONGOLIAN BEEF STEW

One-pot heaven is fall-apart beef that has been cooked for hours in a rich aromatic Chinese-style gravy and blessed by the Holy Trinity of Cantonese ingredients: garlic, ginger and spring onion.

Prep 10 minutes
Cook 2 hours 5 minutes (pressure cooker); 3 hours 5 minutes (casserole)
Serves 2–4

Equipment
Pressure cooker or casserole

550g (1lb 4oz) beef, cut into bite-sized chunks (chuck or brisket)
½ tsp salt, plus extra to taste
½ tsp freshly ground black pepper, plus extra to taste
2 tbsp cornflour (cornstarch)
3 tbsp vegetable oil
2 large onions, sliced
5 dried red chillies
3 garlic cloves, minced
3 spring onions (scallions), cut into 5cm (2in) lengths
1 tbsp ginger paste
500ml (2 cups) beef stock
3 tbsp oyster sauce
2 tsp dark soy sauce

Pat the beef dry with some kitchen paper, then place into a large bowl, season with the salt and black pepper and massage into the meat. Add the cornflour (cornstarch) and toss to evenly coat each piece.

Heat 2 tablespoons of the oil in a pressure cooker or 3–4-litre (13¼–17½-cup) flameproof casserole over a medium heat, add the beef in small batches and fry until golden brown and sealed on all sides. Remove the browned beef and place on to a plate while you cook the rest. Once all the beef is cooked and resting on a plate, add the remaining tablespoon of oil to the pan, then add the onions and fry until softened and slightly golden brown. Now add the dried chillies, garlic, spring onions (scallions) and ginger paste and continue to fry for another 20–30 seconds. Now it's time to add back in the cooked beef and all the juices that will have collected on the plate. Follow with the stock, oyster sauce and dark soy sauce and give everything a really good stir. Turn the heat down to low and place the lid on your pot. Cook for 1½ hours if using a pressure cooker or 2½ hours in a casserole pot.

After the initial cook, remove the lid and continue to cook for a further 20 minutes. Once the beef is visibly falling apart, turn off the heat, check the seasoning and adjust with salt and black pepper if required. If the stew has dried out a bit, you can simply add a little more water and stir through to revive the sauce.

Best served on top of freshly steamed rice or thick rice noodles.

BEEF BRISKET RENDANG

Nothing quite beats slow-cooked red meat. Now combine that with spices and fragrant aromatics from Southeast Asia and creamy coconut milk and you just know this dish is going to be a knockout. Be patient and you can expect to be rewarded with true melt-in-the-mouth moments of happiness.

Prep 5 minutes, plus 30 minutes soaking
Cook 1 hour 40 minutes
Serves 4

Equipment
Casserole or clay pot
Blender

750g (1lb 10oz) beef brisket or boneless short ribs
1 tsp salt
1 tbsp white rice vinegar
3 tbsp vegetable oil
1 cinnamon stick
4 cloves
2 star anise
3 cardamom pods
2 lemongrass stalks, crushed
1 tbsp tamarind paste
1½ tbsp coconut sugar (or demerara sugar)
400ml (14fl oz) can coconut milk
375ml (1½ cups) water
8 makrut lime leaves

For the rendang paste
6 shallots
5 garlic cloves
thumb-sized piece of ginger, peeled
2 lemongrass stalks
6 red bird's-eye chillies

Place the beef in a bowl, add the salt and the vinegar and then cover with water. Allow to soak for 30 minutes; this process will help remove any impurities from the meat and loosen the muscle fibres, ensuring it's tender when cooked.

Once the meat has soaked, drain and place on to kitchen paper to absorb any excess water.

Place the rendang paste ingredients into a blender with a little water and blend until smooth.

Place a 3–4-litre (13¼–17½-cup) flameproof casserole or clay pot over a medium heat along with the oil, then add the blended spice paste along with the cinnamon stick, cloves, star anise and cardamom and fry for a couple of minutes until fragrant. Now add the drained beef along with the lemongrass and cook, turning occasionally, to seal the beef. Once the beef is sealed on all sides, add the tamarind paste and sugar and mix before adding the coconut milk and water. Stir again, bring to the boil and then turn down the heat to low. Add the lime leaves and gently stir in, then cover with a lid and allow to cook for 1½ hours, stirring occasionally. After 1½ hours the meat should be tender and falling apart and the sauce will be thick and sticky. If the sauce is still a little thin, remove the lid and continue to cook, stirring occasionally, until the sauce is reduced and any excess liquid is practically dried up.

Serve on top of fluffy steamed rice.

PORK BELLY AND SALT FISH HOT POT

As little Wans, eating out was something that we would often do with Mum and Dad. It was a way that we could all spend time together away from our own restaurant and just enjoy being waited on, with the added bonus of no pots to wash afterwards. We children would order noodles, sweet and sour and an assortment of dim sum dishes. Dad would order the Hot Pot and how right he was, as the process of cooking this dish in a clay pot locks in the flavour of every single ingredient.

Prep 5 minutes
Marinate 30 minutes +
Cook 35 minutes
Serves 2–4

Equipment
Clay pot or saucepan

250g (9oz) pork belly, skin removed
   and thinly sliced
1 tbsp vegetable oil
2 slices of ginger
2 Chinese sausages (lap cheong),
   thinly sliced
1 onion, thinly sliced
5 dried red chillies, roughly chopped
2 tsp chicken powder
250ml (1 cup) water
100g (3½oz) pre-fried tofu,
   cut into bite-sized pieces
   (available to buy from East
   Asian supermarkets)
25g (1oz) salt fish, thinly sliced
3 spring onions (scallions), cut into
   quarters lengthways

For the marinade
1 tbsp Chinese rice wine
   (Shaoxing wine)
2 tsp light soy sauce
1 tbsp oyster sauce
1 tsp dark soy sauce
1 tsp sesame oil
pinch of sugar
pinch of white pepper
1 tsp cornflour (cornstarch)

Place the pork and all the marinade ingredients in a bowl and massage the marinade into the meat. Allow to marinate for at least 30 minutes but ideally for 2 hours.

Place a 3–4-litre (13¼–17½-cup) clay pot or saucepan over a medium heat, add the oil along with the ginger and sliced sausages and fry for 2–3 minutes, then add the onion and chillies and cook for a further 1–2 minutes. Once the onion has softened, add the marinated pork belly (along with any remaining marinade) and continue to fry for 2–3 minutes. Now add the chicken powder, water and tofu and, once bubbling, turn the heat down to its lowest setting, add the salt fish and cover with a lid. Cook for 25 minutes, then remove the lid, stir in the spring onions (scallions) and cook for another minute.

Serve hot with freshly steamed rice.

HOT AND SOUR BEEF BRISKET

Melt-in-the-mouth beef brisket cooked in a spicy, tangy rich sauce that clings to every ingredient. This stunning dish is well worth the slow cooking process.

Prep 5 minutes
Cook 3 hours 35 minutes,
  plus 20 minutes cooling
Serves 2–4

Equipment
Casserole

1.7–2kg (3lb 12oz–4lb 8oz) beef
  brisket
pinch of salt
1 tbsp vegetable oil
3 onions, sliced
3 garlic cloves, minced
350ml (1⅓ cups) water
250ml (1 cup) chilli bean sauce
125ml (½ cup) white rice vinegar
3 tbsp tomato purée (paste)
60ml (¼ cup) dark soy sauce
100g (½ cup) brown sugar

Season the joint with the pinch of salt.

Heat a 3–4-litre (13¼–17½-cup) flameproof casserole over a medium-high heat, add the oil and, once smoking hot, sear the beef on all sides until caramelized and browned. Add the remaining ingredients and stir to ensure they are well combined. Bring to the boil and then turn the heat down to low, cover with a lid and cook for 3½ hours. Check frequently to ensure the sauce hasn't dried out during cooking and add a splash more water if needed. Turn off the heat and allow to cool for 20 minutes before serving.

PORK BELLY STEW

Packed with porky goodness, loads of veggies and a sour twang from the tamarind, which cuts through the fat so elegantly: this is an abundant combination of taste and texture.

Prep 30 minutes
Cook 1 hour 25 minutes
Serves 4

Equipment
Casserole

700g (1lb 9oz) pork belly, cut into 2.5cm (1in) chunks
1 tbsp white rice vinegar
2 litres (4 cups) water
3 bay leaves
½ tbsp black peppercorns
3 tomatoes, cut into 2.5cm (1in) chunks
1 red onion, cut into 2.5cm (1in) chunks
4 tbsp tamarind paste
3 tbsp fish sauce
3 green chillies
1 mooli (daikon), cut into 2.5cm (1in) chunks
150g (5oz) taro, cut into 2.5cm (1in) pieces
150g (5oz) aubergine (eggplant) cut into 2.5cm (1in) chunks
150g (5oz) green beans, trimmed and cut into 2.5cm (1in) pieces
150g (5oz) bok choy, trimmed and cut into pieces
salt and pepper

Place the pork in a bowl along with 1 teaspoon of salt and the rice vinegar, cover with water and leave for 30 minutes. This process will help remove any impurities and tenderize the meat.

Drain the pork and transfer to a 4–5-litre (17½–22-cup) flameproof casserole and pour over the water. Add the bay leaves, peppercorns, tomatoes and onion, bring to the boil and then simmer for 1 hour with the lid on, occasionally checking for any froth or impurities and skimming these off as the meat cooks.

After 1 hour, add the tamarind paste, fish sauce, green chillies, mooli (daikon), taro, aubergine (eggplant) and beans, give everything a good mix and then cook for a further 20 minutes. Finally, add the bok choy and, after 2 minutes, check the seasoning and adjust to your taste.

Serve in deep bowls with a side of sticky rice.

HONG KONG CURRY BEEF

Sometimes you only have to look at a list of ingredients to know that a dish is going to be outstanding melt-in-the-mouth comfort food. This is one of those dishes: beef brisket, chu hou sauce – which is similar to hoisin with its sweetly fermented flavour – potatoes and coconut milk. SOLD!

Prep 30 minutes
Cook 1 hour 30 minutes
Serves 4

Equipment
Casserole

750g (1lb 10oz) beef brisket
1 tbsp white rice vinegar
1 tbsp vegetable oil
1 large onion, diced
thumb-sized piece of ginger,
    peeled and sliced
3 garlic cloves, roughly chopped
1 tsp Chinese five spice
2 tbsp Chinese curry powder
    (or use your favourite)
1 tbsp ground turmeric
1 tbsp chu hou sauce
1.2 litres (5 cups) water
3 bay leaves
2 tbsp Chinese rice wine
    (Shaoxing wine)
½ tbsp sugar
2 tbsp light soy sauce
500g (1lb 2oz) waxy potatoes,
    peeled and cut into chunks
200ml (7fl oz) coconut milk
2 tbsp cornflour (cornstarch) mixed
    with 4 tbsp water
salt and pepper

Place the beef in a bowl, add 1 teaspoon of salt and the vinegar and then cover with water. Allow to soak for 30 minutes. This process will help remove any impurities from the meat and help loosen the muscle fibres, ensuring it's tender when cooked.

Once the meat has soaked, drain and place on to kitchen paper to absorb any excess water.

Heat the oil in a 4–5-litre (17½–22-cup) flameproof casserole over a medium-high heat, add the drained beef and fry until golden brown, then add the onion, ginger and garlic and fry until translucent. Sprinkle in the Chinese five spice, curry powder and turmeric and mix well, then stir in the chu hou sauce. Once everything is combined, add the water, bay leaves, Chinese rice wine, sugar and soy sauce. Bring to the boil, then turn down to a simmer, place on the lid and cook for 40 minutes.

Add the potatoes and stir into the sauce, then place the lid back on the pot and continue to cook for a further 40 minutes. Once the beef is tender, turn the heat back up to medium and gently stir in the coconut milk. If the sauce is still a little thin, you can add some (or all) of the cornflour (cornstarch) mixture to thicken. Loosen the mixture in its bowl, as it may have set, and stir the pot constantly as you add the cornflour mixture to prevent it clumping. Taste and adjust the seasoning to your taste with salt and pepper.

Serve on top of steamed rice.

RICE BEER STEW

I couldn't write a one-pot cookbook without a nod to a beef in beer stew. I opted for rice beer to honour my East Asian heritage together with several other classic Cantonese flavours, including garlic and spring onions (scallions).

Prep 10 minutes
Cook 3 hours 15 minutes
Serves 4

Equipment
Casserole or clay pot

750g–1kg (1lb 10oz–2lb 4oz) beef, cut into bite-sized chunks (chuck or brisket)
½ tsp salt, plus extra to taste
½ tsp freshly ground black pepper, plus extra to taste
2–3 tbsp cornflour (cornstarch)
3 tbsp vegetable oil
150g (5oz) shallots, peeled and left whole
5 spring onions (scallions), cut into 5cm (2in) lengths
3 celery sticks, cut into 2cm (¾in) chunks
3 garlic cloves, minced
200g (7oz) button mushrooms
5 large carrots, peeled and cut into bite-sized chunks
4 tbsp tomato purée (paste)
1 tbsp Worcestershire sauce
1 litre (4 cups) beef stock
440ml (scant 2 cups) rice beer
3 sprigs of thyme
2 bay leaves

Pat the beef dry with some kitchen paper, place in a large bowl, then season with the salt and black pepper and massage the seasoning into the meat. Add the cornflour (cornstarch) and toss to thoroughly coat each piece.

Preheat the oven to 160°C (325°F).

Heat 2 tablespoons of the oil in a 3–4-litre (13¼–17½-cup) flameproof casserole or clay pot, add the beef in small batches and fry until golden brown and sealed on all sides. Remove the seared beef and place on to a plate while you cook the rest of the meat.

Once the beef is all cooked and resting on a plate, add the remaining tablespoon of oil to the pot along with the shallots, spring onions (scallions) and celery and fry until softened and slightly golden brown. Add the garlic, mushrooms and carrots along with the tomato purée (paste) and Worcestershire sauce and continue to fry for a further 2 minutes. Now it's time to add the cooked beef and all the juices that have collected on the plate, together with the stock, rice beer, sprigs of thyme and bay leaves. Give everything a good stir, securely fit on a tightly fitting lid and cook in the preheated oven for 2½ hours, checking the liquid level after the first 1½ hours. If the stew is looking a little dry, you can add a splash more water and give everything a really good stir to loosen it up again.

After 2½ hours, remove the pot from the oven, place on to the hob over a low heat and continue to cook for a further 30 minutes with the lid off. If you like more sauce with your stew, add a little more water and stir it through the dish to completely combine with the cooked sauce. Once the beef is falling apart, turn off the heat, check the seasoning and adjust to your taste with salt and black pepper.

Serve with a big chunk of bread, rice or potatoes.

THAI PEANUT PORK CURRY

I love peanuts, I love peanut butter and I love curry, so you can see where I'm going with this... quite simply one big bowl of spicy peanut-y love!

Prep 5 minutes
Marinate 30 minutes
Cook 20 minutes
Serves 2–4

Equipment
Casserole or clay pot

350g (12oz) pork loin, cut into
   bite-sized cubes
3 garlic cloves, minced
1 tbsp grated ginger
2 tbsp fish sauce
1 tbsp light soy sauce
2 tbsp curry powder of your choice
2 x 400ml (14fl oz) cans coconut milk
500ml (2 cups) water
250g (1 cup) chunky peanut butter
2 tbsp chicken powder
2 tbsp brown sugar
1 bunch of spring onions (scallions),
   roughly chopped
1 large carrot, peeled and grated
1 lime, cut into wedges

Place the pork in a bowl along with the garlic, ginger, fish sauce, soy sauce and curry powder. Massage everything together and allow to marinate for 30 minutes.

Transfer the marinated pork and any leftover marinade to a 3–4-litre (13¼–17½-cup) flameproof casserole along with the coconut milk, water, peanut butter, chicken powder and sugar and slowly bring to a simmer (do not boil). After 15 minutes of simmering, add the spring onions (scallions) and carrot and cook for a further 5 minutes until the carrot is just tender.

Remove from the heat and serve on top of rice or noodles with a wedge or two of lime.

FISH & SEAFOOD

POOR MAN'S LOBSTER

A celebratory dish (when using lobster) that is always served at Chinese New Year, Christmas and weddings. Well, now you can have it whenever you fancy as the monkfish mimics the taste and texture of lobster tails perfectly, and the slippery glass (mung bean) noodles soak up the rich Cantonese flavours of the sauce.

Prep 10 minutes
Cook 15 minutes
Serves 4

Equipment
Wok

150g (5oz) dried glass (mung bean) noodles
600g (1lb 5oz) monkfish, cut into bite-sized chunks
1 egg white, beaten
100g (1 cup) cornflour (cornstarch)
250ml (1 cup) vegetable oil
2 thumb-sized pieces of ginger, peeled and sliced
1 onion, sliced
6 spring onions (scallions), cut into 5cm (2in) lengths, whites and greens separated
3 garlic cloves, minced
1 tsp sugar
2 tsp chicken powder
250ml (1 cup) water
1 tbsp oyster sauce
1 tbsp light soy sauce
2 tbsp Chinese rice wine (Shaoxing wine)
1½ tbsp cornflour (cornstarch) mixed with 3 tbsp water
2 tsp sesame oil
salt and white pepper

Place noodles in a bowl and pour over boiling water to rehydrate. Once the noodles have softened, drain and set to one side.

Season the monkfish with a pinch each of salt and white pepper and stir through the egg white. Dredge in the cornflour (cornstarch), then bang off any excess and set to one side.

Heat a wok over a medium-high heat, then add the vegetable oil. Once hot, carefully fry the coated monkfish until golden brown and cooked all the way through. This should take 2–3 minutes. Remove and place on a plate or wire rack lined with kitchen paper to drain.

Drain off any excess oil and place the wok, with any residual oil, back on the heat. Add the ginger and onion and fry until translucent, then add the spring onion (scallion) whites and the garlic and fry for a further 30 seconds. Next, add a pinch of white pepper, the sugar and chicken powder and mix well. Then add the water, oyster sauce, light soy sauce and spring onion greens. Once hot, add the rice wine, then give the cornflour mixture a stir and slowly add to the wok, stirring constantly, to thicken the sauce. Turn off the heat and carefully stir in the cooked monkfish and softened noodles. Finally, drizzle with the sesame oil and serve.

XO FRIED RICE
WITH KING PRAWNS

When you think of luxury ingredients, at some point scallops are going to make that list, but have you ever tried dried scallops? Oh, my goodness, they are seriously something else! This isn't just a fried rice recipe; in my opinion this is THE fried rice to beat all others. Juicy king prawns (jumbo shrimp) dancing through toasted fried rice and lavished in dried scallop-rich XO sauce.

Prep 5 minutes
Cook 15 minutes
Serves 2

Equipment
Wok

2 tbsp vegetable oil
350–400g (12–14oz) raw king
   prawns (jumbo shrimp), shelled
   and deveined
1 onion, finely diced
2 garlic cloves, roughly chopped
2 tsp minced ginger
3 eggs, beaten
500g (1lb 2oz) cooked rice,
   chilled (you can use long-grain
   or basmati)
3 spring onions (scallions), finely
   sliced, whites and greens
   separated
4 tbsp XO sauce
salt

Place a wok over a medium-high heat, add the oil and, once smoking, add the king prawns (jumbo shrimp) and fry until they begin to char slightly. Now add the onion, garlic and ginger and continue to fry until the onion has begun to colour. Now pour in the beaten eggs, allowing them to begin to set before stirring gently. Once the eggs have cooked, add the rice and spring onion (scallion) whites and toss gently to combine all the ingredients. Continue to fry the rice for 2–3 minutes; you want the grains to toast slightly, which will give your dish a delicate nutty flavour.

Once the rice is heated all the way through, mix in the XO sauce and, once the sauce is well mixed and the rice hot, turn off the heat. Taste and adjust the seasoning to your preference with salt (XO is quite salty so be sure to taste before adding salt). Finally, sprinkle over the spring onion greens and tuck in.

MONKFISH THAI-STYLE GREEN CURRY

One of the most opulent pieces of fish you can use poached in a creamy, spicy and fragrant Thai-style curry sauce. Best served on top of jasmine steamed rice with a spritz of lime juice.

Prep 10 minutes
Cook 20 minutes
Serves 4

Equipment
Wok or deep-sided saucepan
Blender

1 tbsp vegetable oil
400ml (14fl oz) can coconut milk
600g (1lb 5oz) monkfish, cut into
   bite-sized chunks
pinch of salt and white pepper
3 spring onions (scallions),
   roughly chopped
small handful of coriander (cilantro)
   leaves, roughly chopped
1 lime, cut into wedges

For the curry paste
3 shallots
3 garlic cloves
thumb-sized piece of ginger
   or galangal
3 red bird's-eye chillies
2 lemongrass stalks
1 tsp cumin seeds
1 tsp coriander seeds
2 tbsp light soy sauce
zest and juice of 1 lime

Roughly chop the shallots, garlic, ginger, chillies and lemongrass, then place into a blender with the remaining paste ingredients and blend until smooth.

Place a wok or deep-sided saucepan over a medium heat, add the oil and, once hot, add the blended curry paste and fry gently for 5–8 minutes. Add the coconut milk and bring to a simmer, then allow it to cook over a low heat for 3 minutes. Season the fish with salt and pepper and add to the curry sauce with the spring onions (scallions). Bring back up to a simmer and cook for 5 minutes or until the fish has begun to flake. Turn off the heat and gently stir in the chopped coriander (cilantro) leaves.

Serve with rice or noodles along with a wedge of lime.

BAKED SEA BASS FILLETS

A true nod to my Cantonese style of cooking and to a special dish my dad would cook in the restaurant. Sealing the fish into a parcel guarantees this fish supper will be tender and juicy and packs a punch of classic Chinese flavours.

Prep 10 minutes
Cook 20 minutes
Serves 4

Equipment
Baking tray

1 tbsp vegetable oil
4 sea bass fillets, skin on
thumb-sized piece of ginger, peeled and cut into matchsticks
pinch of salt and white pepper

For the marinade
2 tbsp water
2 tbsp light soy sauce
1 tbsp dark soy sauce
1 tbsp vegetable oil
1 tsp sesame oil
3 spring onions (scallions), chopped into rings
2 red bird's-eye chillies, deseeded and finely sliced
pinch of white pepper

Preheat the oven to 180°C (350°F).

Place all the marinade ingredients together in a bowl and mix well.

Brush oil on to the skin of a fish fillet and then season lightly with salt and pepper. Place the fish skin-side down on to a large piece of foil and spoon a quarter of the marinade over the flesh along with a quarter of the sliced ginger, then carefully wrap the fish in the foil, creating a loose airtight packet. Repeat with the remaining fillets.

Place the parcels on to a baking tray and into the preheated oven. Bake for 15–20 minutes or until the fish is just starting to flake, depending on the thickness of the fillets.

Remove from the foil parcels and serve with steamed rice or rice noodles and drizzled with the delicious cooking liquor.

STUFFED BRAISED AUBERGINE

A classic Hakka dish combining the soft texture of the aubergine (eggplant) with the springiness of the prawn paste, enveloped in rich, smooth oyster sauce.

Prep 25 minutes
Marinate 30 minutes
Cook 25 minutes
Serves 4

Equipment
Wok
Blender

350g (12oz) raw king prawns (jumbo shrimp), shelled and deveined
¼ tsp sugar
¼ tsp white pepper
¼ tsp salt
1 tsp sesame oil
2 tbsp vegetable oil
1 tsp Chinese rice wine (Shaoxing wine)
1 egg
1 tsp cornflour (cornstarch)
2 spring onions (scallions), finely diced
2 large aubergines (eggplants)

For the sauce
1 tbsp vegetable oil
1 garlic clove, minced
375ml (1½ cups) water
1 tsp chicken powder
2 tbsp oyster sauce
1 tsp dark soy sauce
pinch of white pepper
1 tbsp Chinese rice wine
1 tbsp cornflour mixed with 2 tbsp water
1 tsp sesame oil

Place the king prawns (jumbo shrimp) into a blender and pulse until you have a chunky paste – you don't want to over-mince the prawns as small pieces add a nice texture to the dish. Transfer to a large bowl and add the sugar, white pepper, salt, sesame oil, 1 tablespoon of the vegetable oil, the rice wine, egg, cornflour (cornstarch) and half the spring onions (scallions). Mix well until you have an evenly distributed paste. Cover with clingfilm (plastic wrap) and rest in the fridge for 30 minutes.

Cut the aubergines (eggplants) in half lengthways and then cut into 2cm (¾in) thick half-moons. You then want to create a cavity within each half-moon to place your filling (think of an open clam shell). From the skin side, use a sharp knife to cut through each half-moon lengthways, ensuring that you don't cut the whole way through. With a teaspoon, carefully fill the aubergine cavities with the prawn paste; you want it to bulge out slightly.

Once all of the aubergines are filled, heat a non-stick wok over a medium heat. Add the remaining 1 tablespoon of oil and fry the aubergines, prawn-side down, until golden. While the prawn paste and aubergines are browning, combine all the sauce ingredients together, except for the sesame oil and cornflour mixture, and mix well.

Now pour in the sauce mixture around the aubergines. Turn down to a low simmer, place a lid on the wok and cook for 15 minutes until the aubergine is tender. Carefully remove the cooked aubergine from the wok and arrange on a serving plate. Give the cornflour mixture a stir to loosen and slowly add to the sauce to thicken, stirring continuously. Turn off the heat and then add the sesame oil. Pour the sauce over the stuffed aubergines and finally garnish with the remaining spring onions.

EASY CHINESE FISH STEW

This dish was very much inspired by a truly amazing chef I know named Patrick Hetaj. As a Mother's Day treat, I took my parents for dinner and we were served the most amazing fish stew, so I just had to develop a dish that reminded me of this very special occasion.

Prep 10 minutes
Marinate 30 minutes
Cook 20 minutes
Serves 4

Equipment
Casserole

3 medium tomatoes
200g (7oz) monkfish
3 tbsp Chinese rice wine
  (Shaoxing wine)
1 tbsp vegetable oil
thumb-sized piece of ginger,
  peeled and grated
3 spring onions (scallions), finely
  sliced, whites and greens
  separated
2 garlic cloves, minced
1 red bird's-eye chilli, deseeded and
  finely chopped
2 tbsp tomato ketchup
1 tbsp tomato purée (paste)
1.2 litres (5 cups) fish stock
150g (5oz) firm tofu, cut into 2cm
  (¾in) dice
4 langoustines in shell
8 raw king prawns (jumbo shrimp)
  in shell, deveined
250g (9oz) fresh mussels in shell
250g (9oz) fresh clams in shell
salt and white pepper

Score a cross into the top of the tomatoes, cover with boiling water and leave to soak for 2 minutes, then peel off the loosened skin. Once peeled, chop the tomatoes into small dice.

Slice the monkfish into thin bite-sized pieces, place in a bowl along with a pinch of salt and the rice wine and leave to marinate for 30 minutes.

Heat a 4–5-litre (17½–22-cup) flameproof casserole over a medium heat, add the oil along with the ginger and fry for 30 seconds, then add the spring onion (scallion) whites and garlic and, after a further 20 seconds, add the diced tomatoes and chilli and a pinch of salt. Quickly stir to combine the ingredients and fry for 2 minutes.

Stir in the tomato ketchup and purée (paste) and then pour in the fish stock. Add the tofu and gently bring to a simmer, place a lid on the pot and simmer for 10 minutes.

After 10 minutes, remove the lid, turn the heat back up to medium and add the langoustines and king prawns (jumbo shrimp). After 2 minutes, add the mussels and clams and, once the stew is boiling, add the marinated monkfish and any leftover liquid. Gently stir through the stew. After another minute, check the seasoning and adjust with salt and white pepper if required. Finally, turn off the heat and sprinkle in the spring onion greens to garnish.

Delicious served with a hunk of your favourite crusty bread but I heartily suggest you try this with the Chinese fried bread, *youtiao*.

FRIED BANANAS

Growing up in Chinese restaurants and takeaways, we ate a lot of banana fritters, especially on Saturday nights at the end of a very busy service. Dad would cook a big plateful (always drizzled with Lyle's golden syrup) as his way of thanking the staff for their hard work.

Prep 5 minutes
Cook 10 minutes
Serves 4

Equipment
Deep-sided saucepan or wok
Digital thermometer

4 ripe bananas
vegetable oil, for deep-frying
maple syrup, honey or golden
  (light corn) syrup
icing (confectioners') sugar

For the batter
95g (¾ cup) self-raising
  (self-rising) flour
25g (¼ cup) cornflour (cornstarch)
1 egg
1 tbsp vegetable oil
½ tsp baking powder
250ml (1 cup) cold water

Cut the bananas into 2.5cm (1in) chunks.

Place all the batter ingredients in a bowl and mix until smooth.

Heat the oil in a deep-sided saucepan or wok to 170°C (340°F).

Dip the chopped bananas into the batter and then carefully fry them in batches in the oil until golden brown. Drain on a wire rack.

Arrange on your serving plate, pour over your syrup and dust with icing (confectioners') sugar to serve.

WARNING! Allow to cool slightly before eating as the bananas will be extremely hot when they first come out of the pan.

LYCHEE PUDDING

This dessert was a dish we used to eat at my uncle's restaurant. He had a very busy buffet-style restaurant called the Terracotta and this is where I would take my Kung Fu students for a Christmas party. At the end of platefuls of crispy duck, prawn toasts, sweet and sour and noodles, everyone would head to the dessert bar and get several ramekins of soft lychee pudding.

Prep 10 minutes
Cook 10 minutes, plus 4–5 hours setting
Serves 4

Equipment
Saucepan
Digital thermometer

3 (about 15g/½oz) sheets of gelatine
400g (14oz) can lychees in syrup
250ml (1 cup) water
100g (½ cup) granulated sugar
150ml (generous ½ cup) whole milk
100ml (generous ⅓ cup) single (light) cream
fresh lychees, to decorate

Soak the gelatine sheets in cold water until soft.

Drain the lychees and roughly chop into small pieces.

Add the water and sugar to a 1.2-litre (5-cup) saucepan and gently heat to 60°C (140°F) using a digital thermometer. Add the softened gelatine sheets and stir until dissolved, then add the chopped lychees and, using a hand blender, blend until smooth. Now add the milk and cream and mix well. Divide into serving bowls and place in the fridge to set for 4–5 hours, depending on how firm you like your pudding.

Once set, peel and pit the fresh lychees and decorate your serving bowls.

Best served chilled.

ALMOND COOKIES

As a young boy, these cookies were my first-choice treat when we visited the Chinese bakery in Chinatown, London. I'd walk through the cobbled streets leaving a trail of crumbs as I devoured these truly epic cookies.

Prep 15 minutes
Cook 16–18 minutes
Makes 24–26

Equipment
Baking tray

100g (1 cup) finely ground almonds
130g (1 cup) plain (all-purpose) flour
100g (½ cup) caster (superfine) sugar
½ tsp salt
80ml (⅓ cup) vegetable oil
1 egg yolk, lightly beaten
24–26 whole almonds

Line a baking tray with greaseproof baking paper.

Preheat the oven to 180°C (350°F).

In a large mixing bowl, add the ground almonds, flour, sugar, salt and oil and combine to create a crumble-like mixture. Take about 1 tablespoon of mixture and place into your hand, squeeze the mixture together and then roll into a smooth ball, roughly the same size as a small table tennis ball. Then roll the ball to create an egg-like shape. Turn the 'egg' to sit in your palm and then gently flatten it, just a tiny amount, so that the ball will sit on a flat surface. Place on to your lined baking tray. Repeat until all the mixture has been used.

Brush each cookie with egg yolk and gently press an almond on to the top of each one, then place the tray on the middle shelf of the oven and bake for 16–18 minutes or until golden brown. Remove from the oven and leave to cool. These will keep for 7–10 days stored in an airtight container.

MILK BREAD TRAYBAKE

This outstanding sweet bread can really stand on its own two feet. Best eaten in chunks and if you do want a little something to go with it, in my opinion a good dollop of crunchy peanut butter or Nutella are the way to go.

Prep 1 hour, plus 1 hour
  20 minutes rising
Cook 35 minutes
Makes 8 buns

Equipment
Deep baking tray
Stand mixer

800g (6¼ cups) plain (all-purpose)
  flour
9g (¼oz) instant yeast
100g (½ cup) caster (superfine)
  sugar
7g (⅛oz) salt
4 eggs
180g (¾ cup) whole milk
60ml (¼ cup) vegetable oil
1 egg yolk, for brushing

In the bowl of a large stand mixer, add the flour and yeast and combine, then add the sugar, salt, eggs, milk and oil. Turn the mixer on to the lowest setting and combine gently. Once all the ingredients have come together, turn the mixer up a level. Continue to mix for a few more minutes and then turn the mixer up to the next level. Continue to mix until the dough has turned a lighter shade – this can take up to 20 minutes.

Use a scraper to clean down the sides; the dough should not stick too much to the scraper. Turn the mixer back on and continue to mix the dough – it should be very elastic and not sticky. After another 5 minutes, turn the dough out on to a worktop, using your scraper to gather any dough lingering in the bottom of the bowl. Carefully form into a ball; the dough should be quite warm after all the mixing. Cover loosely with clingfilm (plastic wrap) and allow to rise for 20 minutes.

Line a deep baking tray with baking paper.

Divide the dough into 8 equal pieces and, again, cover loosely with clingfilm to prevent it from drying out. To form the dough into a ball, you need to shape and fold it. Take the side closest to you, stretch it over the top of the dough and tuck it under. Repeat this a couple of times, by rotating the dough 90° each time; each ball of dough should have a smooth top. Place each ball into the prepared baking tray, leaving a small gap in between each ball to allow the dough to rise. Ensure you cover the dough at all times when you are not handling it. Once all the balls are formed and in the baking tray, cover with clingfilm and allow to double in size. This should take about 1 hour.

Preheat the oven to 140°C (275°F).

Brush the dough with egg yolk, then place on the bottom shelf of the oven and bake for 35 minutes. Once baked, remove from the baking tray by lifting the baking paper and place on to a wire rack to cool.

Store in a bag (if there's any left) for 2–3 days; ensure the bread is fully cooled before you do this to avoid it sweating.

FLUFFY STEAMED CAKE

Be careful as this sponge will float away if you don't tie it down – I think this might be the lightest, fluffiest cake in the world! No need for a knife or plates in the Wan household, this cake is eaten in tearaway chunks that simply dissolve in your mouth, it's that light and scrummy.

Prep 15 minutes
Cook 25 minutes
Serves 4–6

Equipment
Baking tin (pan) or bamboo steamer
Electric hand mixer

6 eggs
100g (½ cup) caster (superfine) sugar
135g (1 cup) plain (all-purpose) flour
¾ tsp vanilla bean paste

Line a 13–15cm (5–6in) baking tin (pan) or a medium bamboo basket with baking paper.

In a glass bowl, whisk the eggs with half the sugar using an electric hand mixer and, once fully incorporated, add the remaining sugar and whisk again. Place the mixture over a pan of boiling water, ensuring the bottom of the bowl doesn't touch the water, and continue to whisk until the mixture has turned white and creamy.

Remove the bowl from the pan of boiling water and sift in half of the flour. Gently fold the flour through the mixture and then repeat until all of the flour has been added. Add the vanilla bean paste and fold gently through the batter.

Pour the batter into the prepared tin or basket and gently tap on the worktop so the batter fills it evenly to the edges.

Steam on high for 25 minutes.

Allow the tin or basket to cool completely on a wire rack, then remove the lining paper and serve. Any leftovers will keep in an airtight container for 2–3 days.

SWEET RED BEAN SOUP

As a special treat my dad would cook this dessert if we had family over to the restaurant for a get together. He would always cook far too much (on purpose) as the following day we would then fill paper cups with the dessert soup and freeze them. Nothing quite beats a red bean soup popsicle on a hot summer's day!

Prep 5 minutes, plus 8 hours + soaking
Cook 1 hour 40 minutes
Serves 4-6

Equipment
Saucepan
Hand blender

450g (1lb) dried Chinese red beans (aduki)
2 litres (8 cups) water
100g (½ cup) granulated sugar
zest of 1 orange
50g (⅓ cup) dried white tapioca pearls

Begin by washing the red beans, then soak them in water for 8 hours or ideally overnight.

Drain the beans and place them in a saucepan with the water and bring to the boil. Once boiling, turn the heat down to low and simmer for 1 hour. Once softened and cooked, use a hand blender to blend the beans until just broken – you want a few chunks remaining. Now add the sugar, orange zest and tapioca pearls and continue to cook over a low heat for a further 30 minutes.

Serve hot.

EIGHT TREASURE STICKY RICE

We all love rice pudding and this version totally breaks the mould: sticky glutinous rice crammed full of dried fruits, nuts and seeds, sweetened with rich brown sugar and finished with a little tipple of brandy.

Prep 30 minutes, plus 8 hours + soaking
Cook 1½ hours
Serves 4-6

Equipment
Bamboo steamer

360g (2 cups) uncooked sticky rice
10 dried bamboo leaves

For the filling
2 tbsp dried raisins
2 tbsp chopped dried apricots
2 tbsp dried cranberries
2 tbsp chopped pistachios
2 tbsp pumpkin seeds
2 tbsp sunflower seeds
2 tbsp sultanas (golden raisins)
2 tbsp chopped dried dates
2 tbsp brown sugar
4 tbsp brandy

In separate bowls, soak the uncooked sticky rice and bamboo leaves for at least 8 hours or preferably overnight.

Place all the filling ingredients in a bowl, mix well, cover and leave to soak for at least 2 hours or preferably overnight.

After the leaves have finished soaking, rinse off each leaf with clean water.

Drain the soaked sticky rice and then mix through the filling.

Line a 15–20cm (6–8in) bamboo steamer with the pre-soaked bamboo leaves (retaining enough to cover the rice), add the rice mixture and then cover the rice with the remaining bamboo leaves. Place the lid on the steamer and steam on high for 1½ hours.

Serve the sticky rice warm, straight from the bamboo leaves.

INDEX

ACKNOWLEDGEMENTS

Thank you, Jo, for this amazing life bathed in your love; I'm the luckiest boy alive. To the farthest reaches of space, my love. Forever your Wan!

Mum and Dad, I now feed you as you once fed me and it makes me the happiest I have ever been. Thank you for showing me that a full heart and a full belly are all we really need.

Maya and Lola, though you are now both young women, you are, and always will be, my babies. Daddy loves you so much.

DESSERTS